CHINA
AND THE WORLD-WAR

BY

W. REGINALD WHEELER

OF THE FACULTY OF HANGCHOW COLLEGE,
HANGCHOW, CHINA

ILLUSTRATED

New York
THE MACMILLAN COMPANY
1919

Hsu Shih-chang, elected President of the Chinese Republic,
September 4, 1918.

TO
THE BEST OF COMPANIONS
THE BRAVEST OF COMRADES
THE WISEST OF COUNSELORS
MY WIFE

AFTER the war, the attention of the world will more and more shift to China and the Far East. The greatest potential market of the world lies there: the greatest need for industrial and economic development is there. The Far East, in general, and China, in particular, have been profoundly affected by the war: they will be even more deeply influenced during the peace which is to follow. All of the great powers have financial interests in China; after the war, these interests will come into sharp competition and rivalry. In their relations with China and with each other, the nations will face two alternatives: on the one hand, a policy leading to an imperialism and oppression which eventually will endanger the dearly-bought world-peace: on the other, a course of action based on international justice and the development of a democracy in the Far East that will be safe for the world. These alternatives in Asia are, and will be, the same as those which the world is facing in Europe today: the writer believes they should be viewed in the light of the principles for which the larger part of mankind is now fighting and that unless this is done, on the Eastern horizon will surely gather the dark clouds of another world-storm.

In this volume accordingly, the author — who has lived in China for the past three years — has tried to trace the more recent development of this largest of the Asiatic nations, indicating some of the problems which it is now facing, especially as they appear against the background of the world-war, and attempting to point out some of the ultimate issues to which these problems, if they remain unsolved, will lead. To these issues the world at large cannot remain indifferent; and the attempt has been made in this volume to present as fairly and clearly as possible the facts of the present trans-Pacific situation. Throughout the volume, quotations have been made from original documents and statements of the press, in order to avoid, as far as possible, any subjective coloring of the facts. Further, in the interests of international harmony and good-will, the more extreme and less characteristic utterances of the press and of publicists of the nations involved, have been omitted. To this situation in the Far East, it is hoped that the standards and ideals formulated by the free peoples of the world will be applied; and the writer believes that in the application of these standards and ideals will be found a solution — and the only solution — of problems which are of momentous consequence for the rest of the world.

The author desires to express his grateful obligation to Professor F. Wells Williams, of Yale University, and to Dr. John E. Williams, Vice-President of Nanking University, who have given helpful advice, and made valuable criticisms of the manuscript. To the Peking *Gazette,* formerly under the able editorship of Mr. Eugene Chen, the author is indebted for many excerpts from contemporaneous documents and articles of value. Acknowledgment is made of the permission of D. Appleton & Co. to use the summary of *Treaties Concerning the Integrity of China and Korea, and The Maintenance of the Open Door* which appears in Dr. Hornbeck's volume, *Contemporary Politics in the Far East;* and the permission of Dodd, Mead & Co. for the use of the translation of *The Memorandum of the Black Dragon Society,* contained in Mr. Putnam-Weale's book, *The Fight for the Republic in China.* Some of the material in this book was originally published in the *Current History Magazine* of the New York *Times,* and in the *Evening Telegram* of Portland, Oregon; acknowledgment is made of the courteous permission of the publishers to use this in the present volume. In the absence of the author in China, Dr. D. Johnson Fleming has kindly consented to supervise the publication of the book and for his willingness to undertake this task the writer is grateful.

In conclusion, the author wishes to express his appreciation of the services of Miss G. D. O'Neill and her co-workers, of Pasadena, in preparing the manuscript for the press, and his gratitude for the courtesies of his publishers.

Westmoreland Place,
Pasadena, California,
October 1, 1918.

TABLE OF CONTENTS

CHAPTER   PAGE

       PREFACE vii

   I THE ATTACK UPON THE CHINESE REPUBLIC FROM WITHOUT, DURING THE FIRST YEAR OF THE WAR I

  II THE ATTACK UPON THE CHINESE REPUBLIC FROM WITHIN, DURING THE SECOND YEAR OF THE WAR 25

 III THE PROGRESS IN CHINESE REPUBLICAN GOVERNMENT, LEADING TO A NEW FOREIGN POLICY 48

 IV CHINA'S SEVERANCE OF DIPLOMATIC RELATIONS WITH THE CENTRAL POWERS . . 59

  V THE DECLARATION OF WAR AGAINST GERMANY AND AUSTRIA 76

 VI THE LANSING-ISHII AGREEMENT BETWEEN AMERICA AND JAPAN CONCERNING CHINA 102

VII THE CHINESE-JAPANESE MILITARY AGREEMENT OF 1918 127

VIII CHINA'S FUTURE AS AFFECTED BY THE AIMS OF THE ALLIES 145

APPENDICES 184

AN INTRODUCTORY BIBLIOGRAPHY ON CHINA . . 252

LIST OF ILLUSTRATIONS

Hsu Shih-chang, elected President of the Chinese
  Republic, September 4, 1918 . . . *Frontispiece*

FACING
PAGE

An Outpost of Tsingtao, the German Stronghold in
  China 12

Yuan Shih-kai, First President of the Chinese Republic 36

Li Yuan-hung, Second President of the Chinese Republic 54

Feng Kwo-chang, Third President of the Republic,
  and Staff, in Peking, October 10, 1917 . . . 90

Viscount Ishii, Japanese Ambassador to America,
  and Reception Committee in New York, 1917 . 116

Review at Peking of Chinese Troops, a Detachment
  of whom have joined the Allied Forces in Siberia 134

Japanese Troops, in Allied Expeditionary Force in
  Siberia 140

Chinese Labor Battalions ready for Embarkation to
  France 158

Dr. V. K. Wellington Koo, Chinese Minister to
  America, after receiving an honorary degree
  from Columbia University in 1917 172

CHINA AND THE WORLD-WAR

CHAPTER I

THE ATTACK UPON THE CHINESE REPUBLIC FROM WITHOUT, DURING THE FIRST YEAR OF THE WAR

JAPAN'S CAPTURE OF TSINGTAO AND THE TWENTY-ONE DEMANDS

THE Great War first burst forth in Europe, but its effects were felt at once on the opposite side of the globe. These effects were both immediate and far-reaching. Momentous as were the results of the first year of the war in Europe, they were equally significant in Asia, and the making of the new map of the Orient was one of the most important features of the first stage of the great conflict.

On August 1, 1914, Germany declared war on Russia and France; just two weeks later Japan sent an ultimatum to Germany, demanding its complete withdrawal from its possessions in the Pacific. On August 23rd, Japan declared war; within three months, Tsingtao, the Oriental stronghold of the Germans, with the co-operation of a small British force, was captured, and the Japanese were installed in Germany's place in the province of Shantung. Two months later, Japan presented a series of demands on China, divided into five groups, the acceptance of which would have placed China definitely in the position of a vassal state. After less than four months of negotiations, on May 8, 1915, China accepted four groups of these demands, leaving the fifth open for future discussion. Thus, in the first nine months of the first year of the Great War, Germany's political and military power were eliminated in the Orient; Japan had taken over its possessions in China; and China had been forced to concede to Japan extensive territorial rights, economic privileges, and military concessions of great strategic importance. Thus the ante-bellum situation in the Far East was entirely altered, and new problems of international policy and relations were created. The spark struck at Sarajevo had, indeed, kindled a world-wide flame; Europe and Asia, the Occident and the Orient, alike were to feel its transforming force.

In order fully to comprehend the action of both China and Japan during this period, an understanding of their development and international position is necessary. The summer of 1914 found China still in the throes of the attempt to gain political stability within its own boundaries; to make its newly founded republic a stable reality.   Less than three years before, on October 10, 1911, a revolution against the existing Manchu dynasty had broken out; on February 12, 1912, the Manchus signed their Edict of Abdication. A republican form of government had already been set up at Nanking, with Doctor Sun Yat-sen as Provisional President; when the Manchus abdicated, Dr. Sun voluntarily gave place to Yuan Shih-kai, who became the first President of the Chinese Republic.   A provisional constitution was adopted and Peking was chosen as the capital.   Elections to the new National Assembly were held in the following winter and the two houses met in Peking in April, 1913.   Ever since the establishment of the Republic, two clearly recognized parties had been in existence; one composed of the Radicals and the Liberals, made up chiefly of Southerners, with Dr. Sun as their leader; the other consisting of Conservatives and the Military Party who supported Yuan.   The writing of the Provisional Constitution had been done by the Southerners; it limited the power of the President and gave Parliament a large measure of authority.   The majority of the first Parliament were Radicals.   There was much friction between Yuan and the Assembly; it was increased by Yuan's signing, without the consent of Parliament, a loan with the bankers of the Five Powers, including Japan, the United States having withdrawn; by Yuan's expulsion of various Southerners from office; and by the assassination of one of their prominent leaders [1] in Shanghai, Yuan's government being charged by many Southerners with his murder. Finally the President's command to the Military Governor of one of the Southern provinces to give up his office, together with the sending of Northern troops to enforce the order, brought on armed resistance and the rebellion of the summer of 1913. Nanking was captured by the Northern troops and the rebellion collapsed. Dr. Sun Yat-sen and many of his associates fled to Japan. In October the Assembly passed the laws which provided for the election of the President. On October 6th, Yuan Shih-kai was elected President by the two Assemblies for a term of five years; and on the next day, Li Yuan-hung was elected Vice-President. The United States and several South American republics had already recognized the Chinese Republic; now the European Powers and Japan did the same. Thus the Republic acquired a recognized international status.

But the drafting of the new constitution was ac-

[1] Sung Chiao-jen.

companied by more friction, and finally, on November 4th, Yuan purged the Parliament by expelling the Radical members; the National Assembly was dissolved and an Administrative Council was formed in its place. On May 1, 1914, a constitution designated as the Constitutional Compact, which had been drawn up by a conference organized in March, was promulgated. Professor F. J. Goodnow, of Columbia University, who had been appointed Constitutional Adviser, had a large influence in forming this instrument. This constitution gave large powers to the President, granting him practically an absolute veto-power and the right to re-election after a term of ten years. It provided for a One-chamber Parliament. After drawing it up, the Constitutional Compact Conference worked out provisions for a Council of State with the vice-president as speaker, which would act as a legislative body until a new assembly could be elected. This Council of State began its work on June 30, 1914. It had before it the amendment of the laws governing the presidential elections, to make them conform to the new compact; and the laws concerning the formation of the new Parliament.

This, then, was the situation in China at the outbreak of the Great War. From her own viewpoint, her problems were almost entirely internal; her whole mind was bent on the task of building up a republic in place of the old empire. She faced enormous difficulties in the lack of a system of universal education, of adequate transportation facilities, of modern means of industrial production and manufacture, and of any general development of her natural resources. She had to adjust her meagre finances to the pressure and demands of a government of the twentieth century, and she seemed to be tending toward an autocratic government under the guise of a republic. She had little energy to spare for new foreign relations and, when the war broke out, as a matter of course, she at once announced her neutrality.

There was some hope that Chinese territory would not be involved in the military operations of the conflict; but the ultimatum of Japan to Germany on August 15th at once brought the war to China's doors. Japan, in sending this ultimatum, avowedly acted as the ally of Great Britain. The rise of Japan in power and international prestige had been meteoric. In comparatively few years she had broken away from her seclusion; had set up a monarchy in place of a feudal state; and had definitely turned her face toward progress and reform. In this step she was a full generation in advance of China, from which country she had originally drawn her written language, her arts, and much of her civilization. As a result of two victorious wars she had sprung into the front-rank of world powers. In 1895 she had won Formosa and the neighbouring Pescadores Islands from China; Korea had been made independent, and the Liaotung Peninsula, including Port Arthur, had been ceded to Japan. This last territory Japan was forced to return to China on representations of Russia, Germany and France; but in 1905, after the victory over Russia, Port Arthur and the Russian railways and privileges in that section were finally won. All Russia's concessions and powers in Southern Manchuria were given to Japan, and her paramount interests were recognized in Korea. In 1910, Korea was formally annexed. In 1911, at the time of the Chinese revolution against the Manchus, Mongolia became virtually independent, and Japan began to turn her attention to the eastern and inner portions of that province which bordered the Japanese possessions in Southern Manchuria.

In the meantime in Europe, friendly relations were being built up between Great Britain, France and Russia; their community of interests was evident at Algeciras and in Persia. Japan was admitted into this friendship first in 1902, by the formation of the Anglo-

Japanese alliance, which was revised and extended in 1905 and 1911: and, in 1907, in the agreement between France and Japan regarding Far-Eastern affairs, which paved the way for a reconciliation with France's ally, Russia. In 1909, the United States suggested in the interests of the open-door that the Manchurian railways be neutralized but, as an answer, in July, 1910, Russia and Japan entered into an agreement to preserve the status quo [1] without compliance with the American request. Thus in two decades the Japanese Empire had risen to a place of equality among the great nations, and it had gained the power to adapt and enforce her own foreign policy in the world-turmoil produced by the Great War.

The Anglo-Japanese Alliance contained the following stipulations:

" If by reason of an unprovoked attack or aggressive action, wherever arising, either of the High Contracting Powers should be involved in war in defence of its territorial rights or special interests, . . . the other High Contracting Party will at once come to the assistance of its ally and will conduct the war in common and make peace in mutual agreement with it."

---

[1] This was to be followed in 1916 by a Russo-Japanese agreement providing for mutual assistance in case either's possessions in the Far East were threatened by a third power.

When Japan accordingly mobilized its army and its fleet and, on August 15th, sent its ultimatum to Germany, its demands were two-fold:

" First,— to withdraw immediately from Japanese and Chinese waters German men-of-war and armed vessels of all kinds, and to disarm at once those that cannot be withdrawn.

" Second,— To deliver on a date not later than September 15th to the Imperial Japanese authorities, without condition or compensation, the entire leased territory of Kiaochow, with a view to the eventual restoration of the same to China."

A reply within a week was demanded and, none being received, Japan declared war.

Considerable uneasiness was evident in the Orient concerning Japan's ultimate intentions, and several statements were made by Japanese statesmen to allay these suspicions. Thus on the day Japan's ultimatum was delivered to Germany, Count Okuma, the Premier, sent a telegram to the press in America, saying: " Japan's proximity to China breeds many absurd rumours; but I declare that Japan acts with a clear conscience in conformity with justice, and in perfect accord with her Ally. Japan has no territorial ambitions and hopes to stand as the protector of the peace in the Orient." Again, in August 24th, he telegraphed a message to *The Independent* (New York), saying in part: " As Premier of Japan, I have stated and I now again state to the people of America and of the world· that Japan has no ulterior motive, no desire to secure more territory, no thought of depriving China or other peoples of anything which they now possess. My government and my people have given their pledge, which will be as honourably kept as Japan always keeps promises."

On September 2, Japanese troops were landed on the coast of Shantung Province from where they marched overland to Tsingtao. China's fears concerning the possibility of its neutrality being violated seemed justified, as the Japanese army took possession of various towns and cities in the interior, as well as the railroad to the provincial capital; assumed control of the means of communication; and made requisitions upon the Chinese population. A small force of British troops were landed inside the German leased territory and co-operated nominally in the siege of Tsingtao. On November 16, the city surrendered and the German military and naval power in the Far East was eliminated.

Japan now had an opportunity to survey the world situation as affected by the war and to orient itself in relation to it. By the end of 1914 it was apparent that the war would not end quickly: momentous changes in national alignments were in progress; and an unequalled opportunity seemed to present itself in Japan for satisfying various territorial and economic ambitions. As later events demonstrated, these ambitions and aims were five in number. First, to succeed Germany in its position and possessions in Shantung; second, to consolidate the Manchurian territory won in the war with Russia and to add to it a part of Mongolia; third, to gain a controlling share in the iron output of China; fourth, to secure the military safety of Japan by rendering impossible the lease of any of China's ports or coastal islands; fifth, if possible, to enter into such close economic, military and political relations with China, as to make it, with all its vast resources, tributary to Japan. These five aims were expressed in the Twenty-one Demands served on China on January 18, 1915.

The review of these demands by any true friend of Japan is not a pleasant task. It is only fair to say that the liberal-minded statesmen of the Empire, because of the international suspicion aroused, look upon these demands with regret. Every friend of Japan and China hopes that the agreements will be reviewed at the final Peace Conference in the light of the principles for which the Allies are fighting.

Before the demands were presented to China there were various rumours current concerning them. Many Japanese statements were made advocating a more aggressive policy towards China. Perhaps the most important of these was a secret memorandum of the Black Dragon Society (so-named from its connection with the " Black Dragon " province of Manchuria).[1] This statement was by chance disclosed some months after the serving of the Twenty-one Demands. After outlining the world's situation as it affected China and Japan, it emphasized the necessity of solving the Chinese question at once and of forming a defensive military alliance with China, and named most of the objectives which were sought later in the Japanese Demands. It also contained a surprisingly accurate forecast of Japanese foreign policy as a result of the war.

As already indicated in the ultimatum to Germany and in Count Okuma's message to America, Japan had made statements concerning the return of Kiaochow and concerning any attempt to secure more territory or privileges from China. But a change of mind was indicated in December by certain statements made in the Japanese Parliament by Baron Kato, Minister of Foreign Affairs. Having been asked if Kiao-

[1] See Appendix I.

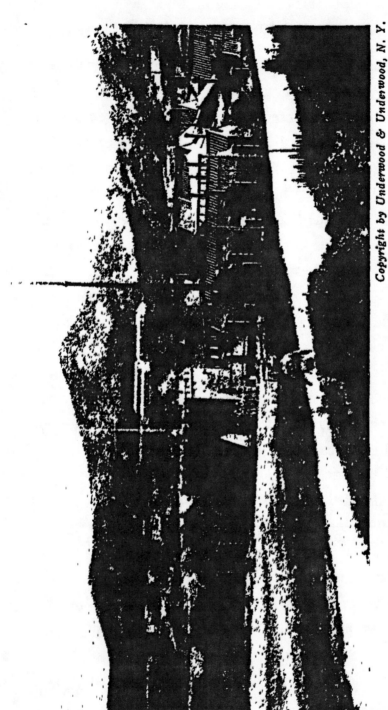

An Outpost of Tsingtao, the German Stronghold in China.

The white buildings in the centre are the German barracks; fortifications and guns are concealed in the hills in the background Tsingtao was captured by Japanese and British troops on Nov. 16, 1914.

chow would be returned to China, he stated that the question regarding its future was at present unanswerable, and further that Japan had never committed herself to return Kiaochow to China. This changed attitude was revealed again in the ultimatum which Japan presented to China in May to force acceptance of the Twenty-one Demands. In this ultimatum Japan used the non-restoration of Kiaochow as a weapon with which to coerce China into an acceptance of the Demands. In the ultimatum, she said in part, " From the commercial and military points of view, Kiaochow is an important place, in the acquisition of which the Japanese Empire sacrificed much blood and money, and after its acquisition, the Empire incurs no obligation to restore it to China." Then, in an accompanying note, she added: " If the Chinese Government accepts all the articles as demanded in the ultimatum, the offer of the Japanese Government to restore Kiaochow to China, made on the twenty-sixth of April, will still hold good." In other words, Japan was holding Kiaochow as a pawn to bargain with, and would continue to hold this territory, unless her other demands were satisfied.

The entire group of requests concerning Shantung, as contained in Group I of the original Twenty-one Demands, was as follows:

GROUP I

" Art. 1. The Chinese Government engages to give full assent to all matters upon which the Japanese Government may hereafter agree with the rights of the German Government relating to the disposition of all rights, interests and concessions, which Germany, by virtue of treaties or otherwise, possesses in relation to the Province of Shantung.

" Art. 2. The Chinese Government engages that within the Province of Shantung and along its coast no territory or island will be ceded or leased to a third Power under any pretext.

" Art. 3. The Chinese Government consents to Japan's building a railway from Chefoo or Lungkow to join the Kiaochow-Tsinanfu railway.

" Art. 4. The Chinese Government engages, in the interest of trade and for the residence of foreigners, to open by herself as soon as possible certain important cities and towns in the Province of Shantung as Commercial Ports. What places shall be opened are to be jointly decided upon in a separate agreement."

The second group of demands dealt with the Japanese sphere in Manchuria and Mongolia: As the result of the war with Russia, Japan had secured a

twenty-five year lease on Port Arthur and control of
the neighbouring railways and Russia's rights in
Southern Manchuria. She was looking with longing
eyes towards Eastern Inner Mongolia, but as yet had
no rights there. Now, in a preamble to this second
group, Japan stated that the " Chinese Government
has *always* acknowledged the special position enjoyed
by Japan in South Manchuria and Eastern Inner Mongolia," and demanded a ninety-nine year lease of Port
Arthur and the important railways of that region; and
privileges of trade and mining and residence in both
Manchuria and Mongolia alike. These privileges
went far beyond any granted in other provinces of
China. They practically transformed Southern Manchuria and Eastern Inner Mongolia into Japanese de-
pendencies. The detailed Demands were:

GROUP II

" The Japanese Government and the Chinese Government, since the Chinese Government has always
acknowledged the special position enjoyed by Japan in
South Manchuria and Eastern Inner Mongolia, agree
to the following articles:—

" Art. 1. The two Contracting Parties mutually
agree that the term of lease of Port Arthur and Dalny

and the term of lease of the South Manchurian Railway and the Antung-Mukden Railway shall be extended to the period of 99 years.

" Art. 2. Japanese subjects in South Manchuria and Eastern Inner Mongolia shall have the right to lease or own land required either for erecting suitable buildings for trade and manufacture or for farming.

" Art. 3. Japanese subjects shall be free to reside and travel in South Manchuria and Eastern Inner Mongolia and to engage in business and in manufacture of any kind whatsoever.

" Art. 4. The Chinese Government agrees to grant to Japanese subjects the right of opening the mines in South Manchuria and Eastern Inner Mongolia. As regards what mines are to be opened, they shall be decided upon jointly.

" Art. 5. The Chinese Government agrees that in respect of the (two) cases mentioned herein below the Japanese Government's consent shall be first obtained before action is taken:—

" (a) Whenever permission is granted to the subject of a third Power to build a railway or to make a loan with a third Power for the purpose of building a railway in South Manchuria and Eastern Inner Mongolia.

"(b)   Whenever a loan is to be made with a third Power pledging the local taxes of South Manchuria and Eastern Inner Mongolia as security.

" Art. 6.   The Chinese Government agrees that if the Chinese Government employs political, financial or military advisers or instructors in South Manchuria or Eastern Inner Mongolia, the Japanese Government shall first be consulted.

" Art. 7.   The Chinese Government agrees that the control and management of the Kirin-Changchun Railway shall be handed over to the Japanese Government for a term of 99 years dating from the signing of this Agreement."

Japan has not a sufficient supply of iron ore; China is rich in this mineral; and the solution was obvious. In Group III the largest iron company in China was to be made a joint concern, and the future mining operations of the Yangtze Valley were to be placed within Japanese control.   The Agreement read:

GROUP III

" The Japanese Government and the Chinese Government, seeing that Japanese financiers and the Hanyehping Co. have close relations with each other at present and desiring that the common interests of the two nations shall be advanced, agree to the following articles: —

" Art. 1. The two Contracting Parties mutually agree that when the opportune moment arrives the Hanyehping Company shall be made a joint concern of the two nations and they further agree that without the previous consent of Japan, China shall not by her own act dispose of the rights and property of whatsoever nature of the said Company nor cause the said Company to dispose freely of the same.

" Art. 2. The Chinese Government agrees that all mines in the neighbourhood of those owned by the Hanyehping Company shall not be permitted, without the consent of the said Company, to be worked by other persons outside of the said Company; and further agrees that if it is desired to carry out any undertaking which, it is apprehended, may directly or indirectly affect the interests of the said Company, the consent of the said Company shall first be obtained."

Group IV involved Japanese control over Chinese coasts, which would ward off any future military measure by another Power. It read:

Group IV

" The Japanese Government and the Chinese Government with the object of effectively preserving the territorial integrity of China agree to the following special articles: —

" The Chinese Government engages not to cede or lease to a third Power any harbour or bay or island along the coast of China."

But the real extent of the Japanese ambitions was revealed in Group V. A new sphere — Fukien — was named, and the right to build strategic railways from the coast up the Yangtse River Valley was requested. In addition, China was to employ Japanese advisers in political, financial and military affairs; police-courts in important cities were to be jointly administered; China's arsenals and war munitions were to be controlled by Japan. These demands, if granted, would have put China definitely in the position of a vassal state of Japan. They were practically the same as the terms forced upon Korea before its annexation. In detail they were:

Group V

" Art. 1. The Chinese Central Government shall employ influential Japanese advisers in political, financial and military affairs.

" Art. 2. Japanese hospitals, churches and schools in the interior of China shall be granted the right of owning land.

" Art. 3. Inasmuch as the Japanese Government and the Chinese Government have had many cases of dispute between Japanese and Chinese police to settle, cases which caused no little misunderstanding, it is for this reason necessary that the police departments of important places (in China) shall be jointly administered by Japanese and Chinese or that the police departments of these places shall employ numerous Japanese, so that they may at the same time help to plan for the improvement of the Chinese Police Service.

" Art. 4. China shall purchase from Japan a fixed amount of munitions of war (say 50% or more) of what is needed by the Chinese Government; or that there shall be established in China a Sino-Japanese jointly-worked arsenal. Japanese technical experts are to be employed and Japanese material to be purchased.

" Art 5. China agrees to grant to Japan the right of constructing a railway connecting Wuchang with Kiukiang and Nanchang, another line between Nanchang and Hangchow, and another between Nanchang and Chaochou.

" Art. 6. If China needs foreign capital to work

mines, build railways and construct harbour-works (including dock-yards) in the Provinces of Fukien, Japan shall be first consulted.

" Art. 7. China agrees that Japanese subjects shall have the right of missionary propaganda in China." [1]

These Twenty-one Demands were rather curiously prefaced by the statement: " The Japanese Government and the Chinese Government, being desirous of maintaining the general peace in Eastern Asia and further strengthening the good neighbourhood between the two nations, agree to the following." They were presented by the Japanese Minister directly to the President, Yuan Shih-kai. The utmost secrecy was maintained and, when rumours became current, the Japanese Government officially denied their existence. A month later, it issued a statement listing only eleven demands, Group V and the more objectional requests being omitted. On April 26th, in place of the original Twenty-one Demands, twenty-four were presented with slightly different wording. On May 7, an ultimatum was sent by Japan, demanding the immediate acceptance of the first four groups and threatening force if a favourable answer was not received. The fifth group was to be held over for future negotiations.

[1] Refers to preaching Buddhism.

On May 8, China submitted, at the same time affirming in a supplementary statement that it was forced to take this step and that it would not be responsible for any consequent infringements upon the treaty rights of other nations or the principle of the " Open Door."

The conclusion of these negotiations marked the winning by Japan of most of its original objectives. The hope of making China entirely subservient had not been realized, but Japan's power over the Republic had been enormously increased and the acquiring of final control seemed only a matter of time. The situation was summed up by Dr. Stanley K. Hornbeck, a leading authority on Far Eastern affairs, as follows:

" Whatever her intentions, Japan has accomplished in regard to China at least five things: she has consolidated her own position in her northern sphere of influence, Manchuria; she has driven the Germans out of their former sphere of influence, Shantung, and has constituted herself successor to Germany's rights; she has given warning that she considers Fukien Province an exclusive sphere for Japanese influence; she has undertaken to invade the British sphere of influence; and she stands in a position to menace and to dictate to the Peking government. A glance at the map of North China will show how completely Peking is at Japan's mercy.   In control of Port Arthur and of the

Shantung Peninsula, Japan commands the entrance to the Gulf of Pechili, which is the doorway by sea to Tien-tsin and Newchwang. In possession of Tsingtao, Dairen, and (virtually) of Antung and Newchwang, Japan thus commands every important port and harbour of the Yangtse. With the Manchurian railways penetrating the heart of Manchuria and the Shantung Railway extending to the heart of Shantung — and with the right to extend the latter line to join the Peking-Hankow line — Japan is in a position, should she so choose, at any moment to grind Peking between the millstones of her military machine. So far as strategy is concerned, Japan has North China commercially, militarily, and politically at her mercy." [1]

The interest aroused among the nations by these negotiations was, of course, keen, and the matter attracted world-wide publicity. The United States was the only great power not involved in the war in Europe, and it was perhaps natural that it should be the one country openly to voice a protest against the settlement. On May 16 she delivered the following note to the Chinese Government at Peking and to the Japanese Government at Tokyo:

" In view of the circumstances of the negotiations

[1] S. K. Hornbeck, *Contemporary Politics in the Far-East*, page 346.

which have taken place or which are now pending between the Government of China and the Government
of Japan and the agreements which have been reached
and as a result thereof, the Government of the United
States has the honour to notify the Government of the
Chinese Republic that it cannot recognize any agreement or undertaking which has been entered into, or
which may be entered into between the Governments
of China and Japan impairing the treaty rights of the
United States and its citizens in China, the political or
territorial integrity of the Republic of China, or the
international policy, commonly known as the open door
policy."

Thus the first year of the Great War brought
changes of the most vital importance to the Orient.
Whether or not these changes shall become permanent
can be decided only at the conference which will come
at the close of the world-conflict.

CHAPTER II

THE ATTACK UPON THE CHINESE REPUBLIC FROM WITHIN, DURING THE SECOND YEAR OF THE WAR

THE ATTEMPT OF YUAN SHIH-KAI TO RESTORE THE MONARCHY

THE first year of the war brought vital changes in China's foreign relations, especially in those with Japan. The second year saw changes within the country of almost as great importance.

These changes, in their ultimate result, were in line with the world tendencies of the present time toward democracy and popular government. Writing in August, 1916, to the New York *Times*, the author tried to sum up the events of the preceding months, saying in part:

" If it were not for the all-absorbing cataclysm in Europe, all eyes would be turned toward the Orient and the great movements now in evidence there. Certainly the developments in India and Japan since the Great War began are of vast importance in the moulding of the future of Asia. But it is in China, especially during the past year, that events of unique interest have taken place. The sudden clamour for the change of the infant republic into a monarchy, which began last fall; the continued agitation for this transformation in the form of government, culminating on Dec. 11 in the unanimous vote of the Convention of Representatives of the Citizens for a Monarchy, with Yuan Shih-kai at its head; the gradual appearance of a most serious opposition, resulting in the revolt of the southern provinces; the sudden cancellation of the monarchial project by Yuan Shih-kai on March 22; the effort to oust Yuan as President, ending dramatically with his death on June 6, and the election of Li Yuan-hung as President in his stead; — these are a few of the main events in a most absorbing, hard-won fight between democracy and autocracy in the Far East. . . . In this fight for the republic in China, America should have a very real interest and sympathy."

The summer of 1915 found China just recovering from the shock of the Japanese aggressions; in retaliation, the country was entering upon a nation-wide boycott of Japanese goods and productions. Attempts were being made to raise a National Salvation Fund to be applied toward strengthening the nation in every possible way. The gifts toward this latter cause were from all classes; one ricksha coolie in a certain city was said to have given to the fund forty Mexican dollars, the saving of his entire lifetime.

Ever since the dissolution of Parliament in November, 1913, Yuan Shih-kai had been moving toward a centralized government, with the power in the hands of a few of his lieutenants. There were open suggestions of a return to a monarchy. The Japanese demands hastened this entire movement. In support of a return to the monarchy the arguments were in the main three: first, that a monarchy, and one of militaristic tendencies, was stronger than a Republic. Germany and Japan were cited as examples. Second, that at the close of the war, if there were not a strong government — if the right of succession were not clear — and if civil strife, which seemed common in a Republic, continued; — the other nations would step in and take control of China and would put a ruler of their own choosing on the throne, just as Japan had done in Korea before its annexation. A third reason was the wish of the eldest son of Yuan Shih-kai to succeed his father as Emperor.

Shortly after the Japanese ultimatum in May, the Chou An Hui (Society for the Preservation of Peace) was organized with the purpose of spreading propaganda in support of the monarchical idea. A pamphlet by a scholar called Yang Tu was circulated in August, giving the reasons for the proposed change. It was entitled " A Defence of the Monarchical Movement," and was in the form of a dialogue between a stranger and a citizen of the Republic. Three excerpts will be sufficient to exhibit its type of reasoning.

" The people of a republic are accustomed to listen to the talk of equality and freedom which must effect the political and more especially the military administration. . . . But the German and Japanese troops observe strict discipline and obey the orders of their chiefs. That is why they are regarded as the best soldiers in the world. France and America are in a different position. They are rich but not strong. The sole difference is that Germany and Japan are ruled by monarchs while France and America are republics. Our conclusion therefore is that no republic can be strong. . . . The best thing for us to do is to adopt part of the Prussian and part of the Japanese in our constitution-making. . . .

" The vital question of the day, setting aside all paper talk, is whether or not China has a suitable man to succeed President Yuan Shih-kai. . . . Confusion and disturbance will follow with great rapidity. Then foreign countries which have entertained wild ambitions, availing themselves of the distressful situation in China, will stir up ill-feelings among these parties and so increase the disturbances. When the proper time comes, various countries, unwilling to let a single country enjoy the privilege of controlling China, will resort to armed intervention. In consequence the eastern problem will end in a rupture of the international peace. Whether China will be turned at that time into a battleground for the Chinese people or for the foreign Powers I cannot tell you. It is too dreadful to think of the future which is enshrouded in a veil of mystery. However, I can tell you that the result of this awful turmoil will be either the slicing of China like a melon or the suppression of internal trouble with foreign assistance which will lead to dismemberment. As to the second result some explanation is necessary. After foreign countries have helped us to suppress internal disturbances, they will select a man of the type of Li Wang of Korea, who betrayed his country to Japan, and make him Emperor of China. Whether this man will be the deposed emperor or a member of the Imperial family or the leader of the rebel party, remains to be seen. In any event he will be a figurehead in whose hand will not be vested political, financial and military power, which will be controlled by foreigners. All the valuable mines, various kinds of industries and our abundant natural resources, will likewise be developed by others. China will thus disappear as a nation." [1]

Here in very glaring terms was shown the fear of attempting to work out a democracy in a world of supposedly militaristic nations. China was afraid to go on with the experiment. The only safety seemed to lie in a reversion to armed autocracy. The Asiatic world was not " safe for democracy," and China had no friend whom she could trust to make it safe for her to continue her attempts in that direction.

All these factors became clear later, but to observers living in China, the political situation in the fall of 1915 was full of mystery. Since the dissolution of Parliament the republic had been one in name rather than in fact; but the speed with which the monarchical movement gained headway surprised most onlookers. The sentiment among the middle and lower classes of the Yangtze Valley and the south seemed strongly against the monarchy and against Yuan Shih-kai for apparently supporting it. The writer talked with men of all classes — ricksha-coolies, Confucian scholars, Buddhist priests, and returned students, and every one, after taking due precaution against being overheard, came out in support of the republic and denounced

[1] Putnam-Weale, *The Fight for the Republic in China*, pages 151 and 161.

Yuan. Dr. Morrison, after a tour of inspection of the Yang-tse Valley, described the sentiment of the people as one of " solid resentment " against the whole movement. The feeling was even stronger in the south.

There were certain indications even then that Yuan Shih-kai was acquiescent in, if, indeed, not a supporter of, the monarchical movement. Persistent rumours came from close friends of his in the capital that he was influenced by his son to make the change for the latter's benefit as his successor. Only former officials and friends of the administration were allowed to vote in December. The editor of one of the Monarchist newspapers in Shanghai, which was blown up by the Republicans, stated outright amid the smoking ruins of his office that he had special permission from the Central Government for his propaganda. But the publication by the Republican Government in the following summer of over sixty secret communications of Yuan Shih-kai's Government preceding and during the election in the Fall brought out clearly the entire situation; the whole monarchical effort, in the words of Putnam Weale of Peking, was stamped as " a cool and singular plan to forge a national mandate which has few equals in history."

In publicly beginning its propaganda in August, following the publishing of the pamphlet by Yang Tu, the monarchical movement very cleverly used a statement of Dr. Francis J. Goodnow, President of Johns Hopkins University, and political adviser to the Chinese Government. Dr. Goodnow's opinion was purely an academic one; he stated that a change from a republic to a monarchy could be successfully made under three conditions: first, that the peace of the country was not thereby imperiled; second, that the laws of succession should first be securely fixed; third, provision should be made for some form of constitutional government. Of course, the Monarchists, in quoting this opinion, entirely omitted these conditional clauses.

On Aug. 16 the *Chou An Hui* published its first manifesto referring to this statement. Yuan Shih-kai, in a speech before the State Council, said among other things: "I regard the proposed change as unsuitable to the circumstances of the country." But on Aug. 30 the first secret telegram was dispatched from Peking concerning the proposed change of government. It was a code telegram to the Military and Civil Governors of the provinces, to be deciphered personally by them with the Council of State code. After certain initial steps are mentioned in detail, the document reads:

" The plan suggested is for each province to send ir a separate petition, the draft of which will be made ir

Peking and wired to the respective provinces in due
course. . . . You will insert your own name as well
as those of the gentry and merchants of the province
who agree to the draft. These petitions are to be
presented one by one to the Legislative Council as soon
as it is convoked. At all events, the change in the
form of the State will have to be effected under colour
of carrying out the people's will." [1]

The Monarchical Society, realizing that matters had
progressed sufficiently by this time for it to assert
itself, on Sept. 27, under the leadership of Yang Tu
and Sun Yu-chun, dispatched a code telegram to the
Military and Civil Governors, asserting that all danger
of a true expression of provincial wishes must be erad-
icated. The telegram offers suggestions regarding the
government of the different districts and then con-
cludes:

" In order to clothe the proceedings with an appearance of regularity, the representatives of the districts,
though they are really appointed by the highest military and civil officials of the province, should still be

[1] The telegrams and communications quoted in this chapter appear in full in a publication of the Republican Government of
China with the title: " The People's Will: An Exposure of the
Political Intrigues at Peking Against the Republic of China," and
in the columns of the *Peking Gazette*.

nominally elected by the districts. As soon as the representatives of the districts have been appointed, their names should be communicated to the respective district magistrates, who are to be instructed to draw up the necessary documents in detail, and to cause a formal election to be held. Such documents should, however, be properly antedated."

On Sept. 29 Chu Chi-chun, Military Governor of Mukden, representing the Administrative Council, telegraphed as follows:

" While the plan of organization is determined by the Administrative Council, the carrying out of the ulterior object of such plan rests with the superintendents in chief of the election. They should, therefore, assume a controlling influence over the election proceedings and utilize them to the best advantage. The representatives of the citizens should be elected, one for each district wherever possible, from among the officials who are connected with the various Government organs in the provincial capital, so that there may be no misunderstanding as to the real object of voting."

This telegram indicated that the representative organ of the people was under the control of high officials and was " utilized " by them " to the best advantage," and that the representatives themselves were to be chosen from among those connected with the Government organizations in the various provincial capitals.

On October 11 the National Convention Bureau sent the following telegram:

"The future peace and safety of the nation depend upon the documents exchanged between the Government organs and Peking and those in the provinces. Should any of these come to the notice of the public, the blame for failure to keep official secrets will be laid upon us. Moreover, as these documents concern the very foundation of the State, they will, in case they become known, leave a dark spot on the political history of our country. Upon their secrecy depends our national honour and prestige in the eyes of both our own people and foreigners. . . . We hope you will appoint one of your confidential subordinates to be specially responsible for the safe custody of the secret documents."

Despite the increasing unrest among the people, a circular telegram was dispatched on Oct. 23, which apparently "drove the last nail into the coffin of the Chinese Republic." It was a nomination of Yuan Shih-kai, and read:

"The letters of nomination to be sent in after the form of state shall have been put to the vote, must contain the following words: 'We, the citizens' representatives, by virtue of the will of the citizens, do hereby respectfully nominate the present President Yuan Shih-kai as Emperor of the Chinese Empire, and invest him to the fullest extent with all the supreme sovereign rights of the State. He is appointed by Heaven to ascend the Throne and to transmit it to his heirs for ten thousand generations.' These characters, forty-five in all, must not be altered on any account.

" Before the form of the State has been settled, the letters of nomination must not be made public. A reply is requested."

A few days later — Oct. 28 — the attention of the Central Government was drawn by Japan, England, and Russia (later supported by France and Italy as allies) toward the inadvisability of taking steps that would threaten the peace of China; but Lu Cheng-hsiang, Minister of Foreign Affairs, replied that it was too late to retract, as the matter had already been decided. When their surprise over this unexpected reply had subsided, those in charge of the plot sent the following state telegram to the provinces:

" A certain foreign power, under the pretext that the Chinese people are not of one mind and that troubles are to be apprehended, has lately forced Eng-land and Russia to take part in tendering advice to China. In truth, all foreign nations know perfectly

Yuan Shih-kai, First President of the Chinese Republic.

well that there will be no trouble, and they are obliged to follow the example of that power. If we accept the advice of other powers concerning our domestic affairs and postpone the enthronement, we should be recognizing their right to interfere. Hence, action should under no circumstances be deferred. When all the votes of the provinces unanimously recommending the enthronement shall have reached Peking, the Government will, of course, ostensibly assume a wavering and compromising attitude, so as to give due regard to international relations. The people, on the other hand, should show their firm determination to proceed with the matter at all costs, so as to let the foreign powers know that our people are of one mind. If we can only make them believe that the change of the republic into a monarchy will not in the least give rise to trouble of any kind, the effects of the advice tendered by Japan will ipso facto come to naught." [1]

On Dec. 21 was played the last act in the drama. Forty-eight hours before General Tsai Ao threw down the gauntlet in Yunnan, because of the strange quiet that pervaded the country the Monarchists boldly determined to pay no further heed to any suggestion that

[1] There is evidence for the view that Japan at first encouraged Yuan in his monarchical aspirations, and then suddenly reversed its position.

they withdraw from their purpose, even though force be threatened. For it had been discovered, after the ballot boxes were opened on Dec. 11 that every voter had cast his ballot for Yuan Shih-kai to be Emperor! And he, isolated in his palace from the populace and deceived by his followers, had accepted the nomination.

All that remained now was to blot out every trace of the conspiracy, that the deceit " should not stain the opening pages of the history of the new dynasty," as a later telegram read, which is in part quoted below:

" No matter how carefully their secrets may have been guarded (it asserts), still they remain as permanent records which might compromise us; and in the event of their becoming known to foreigners we shall not escape severe criticism and bitter attacks, and, what is worse, should they be handed down as part of the national records, they will stain the opening pages of the history of the new dynasty. The Central Government, after carefully considering the matter, has concluded that it would be better to sort out and burn the documents so as to remove all unnecessary records and prevent regrettable consequences. For these reasons you are hereby requested to sift out all telegrams, letters, and dispatches concerning the changes in the form of the State, whether official or private, whether received from Peking or the provinces (excepting those required by law to be filed on record), and cause the same to be burned in your presence."

Such intrigues were certain to bear fruit, and on Dec. 23, Tsai Ao and Tang Chi-yao, Governors of Yunnan, revolted, and blazed the way for the rebellion which ultimately should oust Yuan from power. They declared that Yuan had been guilty of "deliberately misrepresenting the people's will by inducements and threats," and took their stand once more for the republic.   Yunnan was followed by Kweichow.

Despite· this protest, the beginning of the new dynasty [1] was set for January 1, 1916, and the Government buildings in the larger cities were decorated with the national flag in honour of the event. Memorials praying for an early ascension of the throne were sent to Peking by various Monarchists. But on January 26, Yuan Shih-kai, dubbed the "Ta Huang Ti" ("Great Emperor") by the Peking *Gazette,* a Republican sympathizer, announced that the enthronement would be postponed: "The Province of Yunnan is opposing the Central Government and under some pretext a rebellion has been raised in these regions. . . . We are profoundly grieved to confess that a portion of the people are dis-

[1] Called Hung Hsien.

satisfied with us. . . . To perform the ceremony of enthronement at this juncture would, therefore, set our heart on thorns. The enthronement will have to be postponed to a date when the affairs in Yunnan are again under control."

The month of February was one of speculation and of discouragement on the part of the Republicans. The control of the military forces of the north was tightened in all suspected centres; Nanking, which had been the hotbed of revolution for the last four years, was practically under martial law; soldiers with fixed bayonets patrolled the streets; signs were put up in the tea houses and Government schools forbidding any discussion of political affairs; infractions of this rule were severely punished. But the unrest continued, a statement of one of the scholars in Nanking being indicative of public sentiment in general. On being asked by the author what he thought of the new flag which the Monarchists proposed for the nation, he said he thought the best design would be a white flag with a great black spot in the centre (for Yuan Shih-kai).

This dissatisfaction found active expression in the revolt on March 17 of Kuangsi, which made, among others, the following demands upon the Central Government: The cancellation of the empire and reinstitution of the republican form of government; the abdication of Yuan Shih-kai; and the convocation of a legislative body which should represent and be capable of expressing the authentic " will of the.people."

On March 22 this was answered by a mandate from Yuan cancelling the whole monarchical movement. In it he said: " I am still of the opinion that the designation petitions submitted are unsuited to the demands of the time, and the official acceptance of the imperial throne is hereby cancelled. . . . I now confess that the faults of the country are the result of my own faults."

Although Yuan had relinquished his ambition for the throne, he was not willing to abdicate entirely, and nothing short of this would satisfy the Southerners. Chekiang Province revolted and its Governor fled; Kwangtung followed. The press was full of fiery articles calling for Yuan's retirement. On April 27 General Tsai Ao, the great military leader of the Republicans, sent a long telegram to Peking urging Yuan to retire, and concluding with a threat: " If, however, you should continue to linger and delay to make a prompt decision in the sense of retirement and compel the people to elaborate their demands in plainer language, your retirement will be compulsory instead of voluntary, and your high virtue will be lowered." This was followed by a similar appeal by Dr. Wu Ting-fang.

Yuan remaining obdurate, on May 10 the southern provinces elected Li Yuan-hung as President. On May 17 Liang·Chi-chao, the Republican leader, who had the highest reputation among the scholars of China, telegraphed Peking: "Since Hsaing-Cheng (Yuan Shih-kai) has been morally defeated in the eyes of Chinese as well as foreigners, the iron verdict has been passed on him demanding his retirement." This was backed on May 18, the following day, by a statement of 300 members of the former National Assembly, which Yuan had dissolved in 1913.

Through all this discussion Nanking had remained neutral. On May 15 General Feng Kuo-chang held a conference of the representatives of the ten provinces which were still loyal. The conference accomplished little except to emphasize the growing demand for Yuan's retirement. On May 24 Szechuan revolted, and two days later Yuan first publicly announced his intention to retire, saying: "My wish to retire is my own and originated with myself. I have not the slightest idea of lingering with a longing heart at my post." On May 29 Yuan issued a long statement in which he reviewed in detail his action in connection with the attempted change of Government. Two sentences are rather interesting in the light of the present knowledge of the entire situation:

" I, the great President, have done everything I
could to ascertain the real will of the people by taking
measures to prevent every possible corruption, the
same being in pursuance of my wish to respect the will
of the people. . . . In dealing with others I, the great
President, have always been guided by the principle of
sincerity."

The comment upon this mandate by the editor of
the Peking *Gazette,* himself a Chinese, is indicative of
the sentiment of the country at that time:

" If there were not a growing danger with every day
that the Chief Executive tarried in office, moderate
Chinese might be inclined to read with some patience
and in a sense of sympathy the mandate issued on
Monday night, which we translate in full today.   It is
obviously the attempt of Yuan Shih-kai to set himself
right with posterity and to state for the future his-
torian his own version of a transaction that has made
him weaker than the child-ruler who preceded him.
There is no time to reread what has already been as-
severated time and again to a skeptical world.   There
is no time to shed a tear for a fall from greatness that
is without parallel in history.   The nation's perils
thicken and the voice of the people clamours for the
retirement that is to bring surcease of their harass-
ment.   Again we bid him be wise and leave the work

that must be done by other hands under surer knowledge of the great new forces in our midst."

During the following week Yuan Shih-kai became seriously ill, and on June 6 he died, the cause of his death being urinaemia. A few hours before his death he issued his last mandate, in which he handed over the Government to the Vice-President. His closing words were not without pathos: " Owing to my lack of virtue and ability, I have not been able fully to transform into deed what I have desired to accomplish; and I blush to say I have not realized one-ten-thousandth part of my original intention to save the country and the people. . . . I was just thinking how I could retire into private life when illness has suddenly overtaken me. . . . The ancients once said, ' It is only when the living do try to become strong that the dead are not dead.' This is also the wish of me, the great President."

President Li Yuan-hung at once entered upon his office, beginning on June 7, according to the Peking *Gazette,* " the work that ought to have been begun four years ago." His first mandate was as follows:

I

" Yuan-hung has assumed the office of President on this the 7th day of the sixth month. Realizing his lack of virtue, he is extremely solicitous lest something may miscarry. His single aim will be to adhere strictly to law for the consolidation of the republic and the moulding of the country into a really constitutionally administered country. May all officials and people act in sympathy with this idea and with united soul and energy fulfil the part that is lacking in him. This is his great hope."

The issuing of the mandate was followed by telegrams from most of the provinces, stating their loyalty to the new President and to the Republican Government. A few days later Liang Shih-yi, the chief counsellor and adviser of Yuan Shih-kai among the Monarchists, resigned from his position in the Government; thus the chief obstacle to harmony was removed. The efforts of the new Republican Government were then directed toward the establishment of a Parliament, according to the Provisional Constitution adopted at Nanking in 1912. The Constitutional Compact adopted in May, 1914, was discarded. Parliament was reconvened on August 1, and the following month a Cabinet was formed with Tuan Chi-jui as Premier. Feng Kwo-chang was elected Vice-President. Thus the Republic of China again took up its course as a national entity.

The first year of the war had brought grave dangers

to the Chinese Republic from without. In the second year it encountered equally grave dangers from within. The overthrow of militarism, for a time at least, within its own borders, prepared the way for a more sympathetic understanding of the great world situation in which a similar principle was at stake. In its best ideals and traditions China had always been an opponent of military power unfettered by the will of the people. The right of rebellion against tyrants had brought to a close many of its ancient dynasties. The scholar had stood the highest in the social scale: the soldier the lowest. The Confucian Classics, which have had a greater influence than any other writing in moulding the mind of the people, contain many passages emphasizing the importance of the government being founded on the popular will, and designating the ruler as a servant of the people. " In a state, the people are most important: the ruler is of least importance." " Heaven (or God) sees as my people see: Heaven (or God) hears as my people hear." " The commander of the forces of a large state may be carried off, but the will of even the humblest of its subjects cannot be taken from him." In the Analects, the essentials of government had been named: imperfect as was the comprehension of the average Chinese in 1915–16 of all that democracy and popular government meant, there seemed to have been some glimmering understanding concerning the principles at stake: principles which were named by the Great Sage of China over twenty-four hundred years ago.

Tsze-kung asked about Government. The Master (Confucius) said, " The essentials of Government are that there be sufficient food, sufficient military equipment, and the confidence of the people in their rulers."

Tsze-kung said: " If it cannot be helped, and one of these must be dispensed with, which of the three should be foregone first? "

" The military equipment," said the Master.

Tsze-kung again asked: " If it cannot be helped, and one of the remaining two must be dispensed with, which of them should be foregone? "

The Master answered: " Part with the food. For, from of old, death has been the lot of all men; but if the people have no faith in their rulers, the State cannot stand." [1]

[1] *Analects of Confucius,* Book 12, Chapter 7.

CHAPTER III

THE PROGRESS OF CHINESE REPUBLICAN GOVERNMENT LEADING TO A NEW FOREIGN POLICY

On the third anniversary of the outbreak of the Great War, Parliament was re-convened in China, and a new start was made upon Republican paths. Following the death of Yuan Shih-kai in June, Li Yuanhung had been made President; Feng Kwo-chang, Governor of Kiangsu Province, and recognized leader of the Yangtze Valley region, had been elected Vice-President; and General Tuan Chi-jui, appointed Premier of the Cabinet, which was organized in September. On Sept. 15th, Parliament set to work on the drafting of the permanent constitution. The Chinese ship of state seemed to be sailing on comparatively smooth waters. This calm was not broken until the bursting of the storm over the declaration of war with Germany and Austria eight months later.

The general satisfaction over the progress in constitutional government is shown by a description of state affairs sent to America by the writer on Feb. 11, 1917.

" Hangchow, China.

" The prophecy made in verse by Rudyard Kipling concerning the fate of the man who should try to ' hustle the East ' is fast becoming an anachronism.   It is especially inapplicable to the evolution of the government of China.   A year ago the infant republic apparently had been strangled and a monarchy reared in its stead; January 1, 1916, was set as the beginning of the new dynasty with Yuan Shih-kai at its head; and preparations were being made for the enthronement; no discussion of political affairs was allowed, signs forbidding it being put up in all public places.   A protest against the monarchy by Liang Chi-chao, one of the chief Republican leaders, involved him, as he himself admitted, ' in serious difficulties, exposing his life to grave dangers.'   Now, however, all this is changed. The republic has been re-established, Parliament having been in session over seven months; Yuan Shih-kai is dead, and President Li Yuan-hung is at the head of the Government; the draft constitution for the republic has passed the first reading, with its articles guaranteeing freedom of speech and freedom of worship; Liang Chi-chao himself has visited Peking where he was honoured as few Chinese have been honoured by their countrymen.   A concrete illustration of the comparative strength of Yuan Shih-kai's government and the present one is afforded by the situation in this city of Hangchow, the capital of Chekang Province. Ten months ago following the lead of Yunnan, Kwei-chow, and Kuangsi, Chekiang revolted against Yuan Shih-kai and declared itself in favour of a real republic. The Governor, who was a friend of Yuan, was forced to flee; and all connection with Peking was severed. Today as a result of a minor quarrel among the Hang-chow officials, the central Government has sent down its own appointee, Yang Shan-teh, as Governor, and he has been accepted by the people without disturbance. This is the first time that an outside representative of the central Government has been Governor of Che-kiang, and in the judgment of experienced foreigners, his acceptance by the people is a valuable indication of the strength of the present government. In the words of Putnam Weale, of Peking, 'President Li Yuan-hung's seven months' quiet tenure of office has indeed brought the prospects of ultimate success much nearer than it was at any time under Yuan Shih-kai's so-called iron rule, proving conclusively that in civil-ized communities, reason has many times the value of that disruptive and criminal agency,— force.'

"The whole political situation, marking the emer-gence of China from the realm of mediaeval, autocratic government into that of modern, representative government, is a drama of intense interest. The Chinese are passing through the same stages in political philosophy that America and France and other democratic nations have traversed. They are settling now their " Magna Charta " and their " Bill of Rights." The discussion of the constitution was begun on September 15, with C. T. Wang, whom I knew at Yale, now the Vice President of the Senate, as Chairman of the Preliminary Examination meetings. The first reading was finished and a report made on January 19th. The eleven original chapters and several additional ones were discussed. The chapters concerning the " form of State," that of a republic; the rights of citizens, including freedom of speech, and freedom of worship; the two-house system of parliament; the appointment of a Premier and Cabinet; the organization of law courts; were all passed by the necessary three-quarter vote of the quorum made up of two-thirds membership of the two houses."

There were three subjects which aroused special discussion at the Capital. They were the budget, local self-government and State religion. The matter of finance was always a trying one, as China had to rely largely on foreign loans. The money advanced by America was generally welcomed, and the announcement that America intended to encourage investment in China was greeted with satisfaction.

The provincial self-government bill was passed in the first reading January 10th after much discussion, and the President issued a mandate supporting it. He said in part:

"In the olden days the district and prefect system formed the beginning of an excellent system of government, and the services of the village elders and district councillors were reported as valuable aids to good administration. The spirit of self-government had therefore already been developed in ancient times. . . . In the Tsing Dynasty a beginning was made in self-government, and a system far from complete and satisfactory was set up. When the republic was formed the work was continued . . . and at this time of general reform, when it is necessary to build up a strong foundation of democratic administration, we should draw up a suitable system, and enforce the same within a definite time limit. . . . By such a system we may reach the stage of universal peace. This is my ambitious hope."

The question of a state religion was brought up in connection with Chapter Three of the Constitution, guaranteeing religious liberty for all. An article of that chapter stated that the Confucian ethics should be used as a basis in primary education. A movement was started among the older, conservative members of Parliament to have Confucianism as a state religion, but of the twenty "parties" or groups in Parliament, a canvass revealed that only four supported this measure, although most of them favoured an emphasis upon Confucian ethics in the school system. During the first week of February the discussion was most lively while this article was undergoing a second reading. Various arguments were advanced on either side, several of them sounding rather strange in the ears of foreigners. Some of the points in favour of Confucianism were: (1) The great influence of Confucius in China in the past and present; (2) the foreign-mission schools teach the "Four Books" of Confucius; (3) most of the Western Nations have discarded Christianity; and China should not seek to pick it up. Against the measure: (1) Confucius was a teacher of ethics, not religion; (2) his teaching has more to do with the sovereign than the people, and is not fitting for a republic; (3) a state religion was not republican; (4) such a measure would conflict with the chapter on religious freedom. Finally, on February 9th it was voted to cease discussion, and five different amendments advocating a state religion were defeated. The

Peking Gazette, edited by a young progressive Chinese, commented thus upon the meeting:

" Yesterday's meeting of the Conference on Constitution was historic for the reason that the question whether the Republic of China shall create a precedent, in the history of Republicanism by making one of the many religions, if Confucianism can be called a religion, the State religion of the country, was settled after a long and serious struggle. The Confucianists resorted to every possible means to win but the odds against them were too strong. The question of freedom of religious belief is by no means settled but the attempt to give the Republic a State religion has been definitely defeated."

A few quotations from the native press of the country will reveal the spirit of the people at that time. It should be remembered that a year before practically no expression of public opinion was allowed.

On January 12th the *Min-Kwo-hsin-pao* spoke as follows:

" Coming as we do in sight of the sacred instrument of Government which is to protect us from tyranny and misrule and assure to us the blessings of liberty and democracy, it is fitting that we recall the bloodshed and tribulations through which we have triumphed over monarchy and autocracy. . . . The

Li Yuan-hung, Second President of the Chinese Republic.

mere possession of a Constitution is one thing, and its enjoyment is another. We care for no hollow Constitution, but we are willing to die for a Constitution that is a reality. We know the spirit of our people, so 'Ten Thousand Years' to our Constitution." On January 17th the *Kung-min-pao* expressed itself thus: "We have a Republic but not a democracy. The Republic was established by the revolution of 1911. But Democracy is still in the making. By wresting from the Monarchy our form of government, half of the battle was won; and now we have to bend our energy to training our people in democracy."

On January 27th the *Peking Jih-pao* emphasized the need of moral strength back of all political changes — its message was a thoughtful and valuable one at that time:

"Signs of progress in the country are not lacking. Intellectually the people have taken a leap forward. The idea of democracy and general knowledge of modern learning are gradually being spread among the people. This is a hopeful sign. But knowledge without moral backbone is worse than ignorance. The morality of our people, we are sorry to say, has not kept pace with their advance in knowledge. We are in the same predicament as France was immediately after her great revolution. The people have cut adrift from old traditions, but have not assimilated new ideas and principles rapidly enough to supply the resulting moral vacuum. We can say without fearing challenge that the morality of the people is everything in the life of a nation. While we may be busy instituting reforms and improving the minds of the people, we must not for a minute lose sight of this signal fact — the soul of the nation."

In conclusion, the opinions of two foreigners, one an Englishman, the other an American, concerning the situation as it then appeared, are worthy of quotation. The first is Mr. Putnam Weale, for many years a correspondent in Peking, and author of several standard books on the Far East. On January 16th, he wrote in the *Peking Gazette* as follows:

"The conviction which the writer has consistently cherished, that the situation in this country is as good as could possibly be expected — and gives reasonable promise of peaceful development in the future — seems based on sound premises. . . . The Chinese as a people are temperamentally suited to representative government; they are reasonable, tactful, conciliatory and humorous; four saving graces which will carry them very far along the road to political success. Like a solid piece of iron which binds the nation together is its immense, majestic, abiding common-sense."

At a recent dinner in Shanghai given by the American Consul General, which was attended by prominent Chinese and Americans, the Honourable Victor Murdoch spoke as follows:

" The Republic is here to stay in China; the same brand of democracy which has built up the United States can build up China. . . . I have observed a great deal of this spirit while I have been here in China. . . . Here is a wonderful people, industrious beyond any other people, sober beyond others, good-humoured, and law-abiding. . . . No one can reach the limits of China. China is the place of the future. I have been impressed by everything I have seen in this country, with its promise of future development, but one thought that lingers longest in my mind is this: China's future development and prosperity lie in her form of government. It must be a republic to obtain results. What the old flag has done for America, the Chinese flag can do for the Chinese people. It is a banner of no dynasty but a people's flag, and people who are industrious and sober and self-governing, can endure for ever — and so can the United States and China."

This was the situation in China when the announcement of Germany's unrestricted submarine warfare was made to the World. That policy irrevocably changed the course of the Nations, and brought the American Republic to the brink of war; the great Republic in the Orient was not to escape similar effects.

CHAPTER IV

CHINA'S SEVERANCE OF DIPLOMATIC RELATIONS WITH THE CENTRAL POWERS

AT the outbreak of the World War, as has been related, China declared its neutrality, and bent all its energies to the building up of its newly-founded republic. But before the middle of the third year of the war had passed, it became apparent that the Republic must take some stand in relation to the issues of the great struggle. Four conditions influenced it in this regard. The Republic seemed at last to be making headway toward stability and permanence, and with the new national consciousness came a clearer realization of the principles at stake in the war. Secondly, China desired a place at the Peace Conference which would settle the question of the disposal of Kiaochow and the German interests in Shantung and, as she hoped, would review the Twenty-one Demands. In 1905 in the Portsmouth Treaty, Japan had negotiated directly with Russia concerning Manchuria, although it was a province of China, and China was not admitted until the final decisions were reached. This was a

precedent which China could not afford to see repeated
in Shantung, if she were to continue as a sovereign
state; and so she was ready to make any effort to
gain a voice in the eventual international conference.
In the third place, America seemed to be more and
more turning toward some sort of active participation
in the conflict, and China desired to keep its foreign
policy close in accord with that of the nation which
it regarded as its best friend. Finally, two incidents
in its foreign relations in the latter part of 1917 had
aroused China afresh to a consciousness of its weak-
ness and its lack of international standing. These
two events were the Chengchiatun dispute with Japan
in Manchuria, and the Lao-hsi-kai incident in Tientsin
with the French Government.

Chengchiatun was a Manchurian market-town situated near the Mongolian border. It was of some
importance as a trade centre and had been menaced
by one of the Mongol brigands at the time of the
Manchu restoration. The Twenty-eighth Division of
the Chinese army had been stationed there to protect
the town and preserve order. In August a detachment of Japanese troops was sent there to carry out
manœuvres. Their presence in that portion of Manchuria could be justified only by a most liberal interpretation of Japanese treaty-rights. On August 13,

a dispute arose between a Japanese merchant named Yoshimoto and a Chinese fish-pedlar; the Japanese attempted to punish the pedlar; a Chinese soldier interfered; other soldiers of both nationalities came up; and a mêlée resulted, in which several Japanese and Chinese were wounded and killed. Exaggerated reports were published in the Japanese press and its Government at once took up the matter and demanded a series of privileges and concessions in that region and the neighbouring territory. The first demands were:

1. Punishment of the General commanding the Twenty-eighth Division.

2. The dismissal of officers at Chengchiatun responsible for the occurrence as well as the severe punishment of those who took direct part in the fracas.

3. Proclamations to be posted ordering all Chinese soldiers and civilians in South Manchuria and Eastern Inner Mongolia to refrain from any act calculated to provoke a breach of the peace with Japanese soldiers or civilians.

4. China to agree to the stationing of Japanese police officers in places in South Manchuria and Eastern Inner Mongolia where their presence was considered necessary for the protection of Japanese subjects. China also to agree to the engagement by the

officials of South Manchuria of Japanese police advisers.

And in addition:

1. Chinese troops stationed in South Manchuria and Eastern Inner Mongolia to employ a certain number of Japanese military officers as advisers.

2. Chinese military cadet schools to employ a certain number of Japanese military officers as instructors.

3. The Military Governor of Mukden to proceed personally to Port Arthur to the Japanese Military Governor of Kwantung to apologize for the occurrence and to tender similar personal apologies to the Japanese Consul General in Mukden.

4. Adequate compensation to be paid by China to the Japanese sufferers and to the families of those killed.

These privileges if granted would have paved the way for a Japanese Protectorate over Southern Manchuria and Eastern Mongolia. Negotiations continued during the fall and final agreement was reached on the five following terms:

1. The General commanding the Twenty-eighth Division to be reprimanded.

2. Officers responsible to be punished according to

law. If the law provides for severe punishment, such punishment will be inflicted.

3. Proclamations to be issued enjoining Chinese soldiers and civilians in the districts where there is mixed residence to accord · considerate treatment to Japanese soldiers and civilians.

4. The Military Governor of Mukden to send a representative to Port Arthur to convey his regret when the Military Governor of Kwantung and Japanese Consul General at Mukden are there together.

5. A solatium of $500 (Five Hundred Dollars) to be given to the Japanese merchant Yoshimoto.

This settlement was generally satisfactory to the Chinese; but the original demands had caused them much anxiety, and impressed upon them the necessity of securing a better understanding of their rights as a sovereign power.

The Lao-hsi-kai incident with France was of less importance. The French Consular authorities of Tientsin desired to have their concession extended and had been negotiating with the Chinese Government for additional space. The negotiations had dragged on for some years and a final agreement had been practically reached concerning this additional grant of land which was to be put under the jurisdiction of a joint Franco-Chinese Administration. Some additional opposition was raised by the Chinese, and finally the French Consul-General sent an ultimatum demanding that the Chinese police be removed and the additional territory be placed under French supervision and control. The time-limit of the ultimatum having expired, a French detachment of soldiers took possession of the property; the Chinese policemen were removed and imprisoned; and French sentries were stationed along the boundary. Protests arose from the Chinese of the city and of North China; the native servants and employés of the French Concession left in a body. The arrested Chinese police were ultimately released but no immediate settlement was reached concerning the matter in question. The incident could easily have been averted and was not of great importance, except as it was used by German propagandists, but it served to increase China's desire to be treated as an equal by the European Powers.

For the reasons cited, the country was ready in the fall of 1916 to step out into a more active participation in the world's events, and when President Wilson sent out his peace inquiry of December 19, 1916, China answered at once, expressing its willingness to join in the international effort to eradicate wars of aggression; " to assure the respect of the principle of the equality of nations, whatever their power may be, and to relieve them of the peril of wrong and violence." The note of the Chinese Minister of Foreign Affairs to the American Minister at Peking was as follows:

" I have examined with the care which the gravity of the question demands the note concerning peace which President Wilson has addressed to the Governments of the Allies and the Central Powers now at war and the text of which Your Excellency has been good enough to transmit to me under instructions of your Government.

" China, a nation traditionally pacific, has recently again manifested her sentiments in concluding treaties concerning the pacific settlement of international disputes, responding thus to the voeux of the Peace Conference held at The Hague.

" On the other hand, the present war, by its prolongation, has seriously affected the interests of China, more so perhaps than those of other Powers which have remained neutral. She is at present at a time of reorganization which demands economically and industrially the co-operation of foreign countries, a co-operation which a large number of them are unable to accord on account of the war in which they are engaged.

"In manifesting her sympathy for the spirit of the President's Note, having in view the ending as soon as possible of the hostilities, China is but acting in conformity not only with her interests but also with her profound sentiments.

"On account of the extent which modern wars are apt to assume and the repercussions which they bring about, their effects are no longer limited to belligerent States. All countries are interested in seeing wars becoming as rare as possible. Consequently China cannot but show satisfaction with the views of the Government and people of the United States of America who declare themselves ready, and even eager, to co-operate when the war is over, by all proper means to assure the respect of the principle of the equality of nations, whatever their power may be, and to relieve them of the peril of wrong and violence. China is ready to join her efforts with theirs for the attainment of such results which can only be obtained through the help of all."

Thus China was ready to act, when the German Government threw down the challenge to the civilized world by its declaration of unlimited submarine warfare. 'America severed diplomatic relations, and on February 4th sent a note to China, as to all neutrals, suggesting that they follow its example. In less than a week the Chinese Republic actually took this step. Writing from China on February 16th, the author described the decision as follows:

Hangchow, China, February 16.

" The severance of diplomatic relations between America and Germany has had far-reaching effects in China. I was in Shanghai when the news came and the city, in which there are over 20,000 foreigners, including 1000 Germans, was greatly stirred. Crowds gathered around the bulletin boards, just as they did in Europe during the first days of August, 1914. The English and French were openly elated; the Germans were correspondingly depressed; and the Chinese appeared in doubt as to their action in this crisis. The American gunboats and cruisers in the harbour were loading supplies and coaling, in preparation for departure in case a declaration of war necessitated such action.

" The indecision which at first marked the action of the Chinese and their government, has been cast aside by the decision of the government on February 9, when it boldly followed the course of America by sending a similar declaration to Germany. This action has been greeted on all sides as a sign of the virility of the present republican government, and the first step in modern participation in world affairs.

" After America severed relations with Germany there was serious discussion at Peking of China's future action. The younger element in the government were eager to follow America's example; the older, more conservative leaders counselled caution and a maintenance of neutrality. The most experienced statesmen, including Liang Chi-chao, who is so largely responsible for the present Republican government, were summoned to the capitol for conference. Finally, after an all-day meeting on February 9, decisive action was agreed upon, and notes were sent to Germany and to America. The note to Germany follows:

" ' A telegraphic communication has been received from the Chinese minister at Berlin transmitting a note from the German government dated February 1, 1917, which makes known that the measures of blockade newly adopted by the government of Germany will, from that day, endanger neutral merchant vessels navigating in certain prescribed zones.

" ' The new measures of submarine warfare inaugurated by Germany, imperiling the lives and property of Chinese citizens to even a greater extent than the measures previously taken which have already cost so many human lives to China, constitute a violation of the principles of public international law at present in force; the tolerance of their application would have as a result the introduction into international law of arbitrary principles incompatible with even legitimate commercial intercourse between neutral states and belligerent powers.

" ' The Chinese government, therefore, protests energetically to the imperial German government against measures proclaimed on February 1, and sincerely hopes that with a view to respecting the rights of neutral states and to maintaining the friendly relations between these two countries, the said measures will not be carried out.

" ' In case contrary to its expectations its protest be ineffectual the government of the Chinese republic will be constrained to its profound regret, to sever diplomatic relations at present existing between the two countries. It is unnecessary to add that the attitude of the Chinese government has been dictated purely by the desire to further the cause of the world's peace and by the maintenance of the sanctity of international law.'

" On the same day China, through its Foreign Minister, sent the following note to the American Minister in Peking for transmission to the United States Government:

" ' I· have the honour to acknowledge the receipt of your excellency's note of the 4th of February, 1917, informing me that the government of the United States of America, in view of the adoption by the German government of its new policy of submarine warfare on February 1st, has decided to take certain action which it judges necessary as regards Germany.

" ' The Chinese government, like the President of the United States of America, is reluctant to believe that the German government will actually carry into excution those measures which imperil the lives and property of citizens of neutral states and jeopardize the commerce, even legitimate, between neutrals as well as between neutrals and belligerents and which tend, if allowed to be enforced without opposition, to ·introduce a new principle into public international law.

" ' The Chinese government also proposes to take such action in the future as will be deemed necessary for the maintenance of the principles of international law.'

" The *China Press,* an American newspaper of Shanghai, comments thus upon this action:

" ' The note of warning to Germany marks a bold

and heroic departure from historic precedent for China. It shows that things are moving in the republic, and moving rapidly, and we believe that it will be fully justified by events.' In commenting on the action, the *Peking Gazette*, a native paper, says that ' The decision arrived at is in every sense a victory of the younger intellectual forces over the older mandarinate, whose traditions of laissez faire and spineless diplomacy have hitherto cost China so much.'

" These sentiments are re-echoed in various other native papers that decry ' Prussian militarism ' — and advise China's following America's action. The reasons underlying the decision are expressed fairly well by the *Kun Yuan Pao* in an editorial which appeared under the headline ' Now or Never,' the day before the government acted:

" ' This is the time for action. We must range ourselves on the side of justice, of humanity and of international law. We must also win a place for ourselves, friends, in the council of nations by prompt and decisive action. Now, Germany's submarine policy and the United States' resolute stand against lawlessness and wholesale atrocity have given us the opportunity.

" ' Germany's submarine policy is a challenge to the world. America has accepted the challenge. Shall we do otherwise? If we have a particle of respect for ourselves, the way pointed out by the United States is the road to honour and self-respect.

" ' Then, is it not altogether unprofitable to join the allies if we consider the question only from a national point of view? In the present state of the world, it is impossible for any nation to stand alone. We must have allies, if not so sanctified in treaties, yet in a mutual bond of sympathy. This is the best opportunity for us to win friends among the powers. Possibly we will have only a little say in the peace conference, but since we have been willing to help Great Britain, France, Russia and the United States, our appeal will not be unheeded when we should be in difficulties. Although we have been observing the strictest neutrality in the war, there are many questions at the peace conference which will touch us vitally. There is, for instance, the question of Tsingtao to settle, and the Japanese actions in Manchuria and in connection with the Twenty-one demands will have to be brought up in review. Cultivate friendship when our friends are in need, and not when they are above wants. Now or never must we show the world that this is a nation which is not always on the sick list, but living, pulsating and with a fighting spirit.' "

After the sending of the Chinese note to Germany

nothing was heard from that quarter for several weeks. Then came the torpedoing of the French ship, *Atlas*, on which were over five hundred Chinese labourers. The Cabinet was in favour of breaking off relations, and on March 10th the question was sent to Parliament for decision. The Lower House upheld the Cabinet decision and the next day the Senate did the same.

The long-awaited German answer arrived on the day the Lower House voted. In part it was as follows:

"The Imperial German Government expresses its great surprise at the action threatened by the Government of the Republic of China in its note of protest. Many other countries have also protested, but China, which has been in friendly relations with Germany, is the only State which has added a threat to its protest.

. . . "Germany's enemies were the first to declare a blockade on Germany and the same is being persistently carried out. It is therefore difficult for Germany to cancel her blockade policy. The Imperial Government is nevertheless willing to comply with the wishes of the Government of the Republic of China by opening negotiations to arrive at a plan for the protection of Chinese life and property, with the view that the end may be achieved and thereby the utmost regard be given to the shipping rights of China. The reason which has prompted the Imperial Government to adopt this conciliatory policy is the knowledge that, once diplomatic relations are severed with Germany, China will not only lose a truly good friend but will also be entangled in unthinkable difficulties."

This note arrived too late to have any effect on Parliament, which upheld the decision of the Cabinet as indicated.

The mildness of Germany's note of March 10th was rather a surprise to the inhabitants of China, who remembered the seizure of Tsingtao in 1898, and other actions in Shantung as the result of the murder of two German missionaries; and the ruthlessness of the German troops at the time of the Boxer uprising. A leading Chinese lawyer commented on the change of attitude, his remarks being an indication of the new position won by China in world-politics:

" The troops under Count Waldersee, leaving Germany for the relief of Peking, were instructed by the War Lord to grant no quarter to the Chinese; on the other hand, the latter were to be so disciplined that they would never dare look a German in the face again.[1] The whirligig of time brings in its

[1] It is interesting to note that the armies under Attila were

own revenge, and today, after the lapse of scarcely seventeen years, we hear the *Vossische Zeitung* commenting on the diplomatic rupture between China and Germany, lamenting that even so weak a State as the Far Eastern Republic dares look defiantly at the German nation!"

On March 14th the German and Austrian Ministers and their staffs were handed their passports and the German and Austrian interests were turned over to the Dutch Legation. Thus did China take its first step toward participation in the cause of the Allies.

held up as examples for the German soldiers to follow, by Kaiser Wilhelm in 1900, in his speech to the German troops embarking for China. This was perhaps the first association of the term "Huns" with German forces. The Kaiser's exact words were: "As soon as you come to blows with the enemy he will be beaten. No mercy will be shown! No prisoners will be taken! As the Huns, under King Attila, made a name for themselves, which is still mighty in traditions and legends to-day, may the name of German be so fixed in China by your deeds, that no Chinese shall ever again dare even to look at a German askance. . . . Open the way for *Kultur* once for all."

CHAPTER V

CHINA'S DECLARATION OF WAR AGAINST GERMANY AND AUSTRIA

On March 14, 1917, China severed diplomatic relations with Germany; exactly five months later, on August 14th, she declared war. The strain of reaching this final decision shook the Republic to its foundations, temporarily causing a complete breakdown of the Central Government, and indirectly making possible the brief restoration of the Manchus which took place in July. But eventually the Chinese ship-of-state righted itself and emerged on the broad seas of world-relationships as a recognized member of the league of the Allies.

The breaking off of relations with Germany brought to light the state of discord which had existed for some time between the Premier, Tuan Chi-jui, and the President, Li Yuan-hung. The former was a military leader and had been trained in the Manchu type of government. The latter was a real republican in spirit and had insisted that every act of the State be carried out according to the existing Constitution. The Premier desired to break off relations without consulting Parliament; the President insisted on the latter step, and after Tuan had threatened to resign, and had actually left the capital for Tientsin, the President persuaded him to return and to present the question to Parliament. This was done with the result already indicated.

Having taken two steps, the next move was to declare war. Here, however, appeared many difficulties. It is hard for a foreigner to judge Chinese public opinion, but after a trip through the coast cities into the interior, the following arguments for and against the declaration seemed to the writer to be involved.[1]

The reasons in favour of the declaration seemed to be four in number. First, the intelligent Chinese sympathized deeply with the cause of the Allies, especially in their championing the rights of small or weak nations, with the protection of such countries from aggression and the assurance to them of the right to work out their own destinies unafraid. This formula seemed to fit the facts of China's relationships in the Orient. She was trying to build up a republic; she

[1] An interesting account of events in Peking preceding the war declaration is given in an article by Carson Chang, Secretary to the President, entitled " The Inside History of China's Declaration of War," *Millard's Review*, Aug. 17, '18.

had made many costly mistakes; but ultimate success seemed possible if she could be protected from attack by predatory powers. The Allies promised such protection to all such weak nations, and China could not but be in sympathy with their aims.

Secondly, China desired a place in the Peace Conference which would be held at the close of the war. There were many questions affecting its own territory and rights which would come up then, and China desired a voice in their settlement. The German rights in Shantung which seemed likely to fall to Japan; the subject of the Twenty-one Demands; the future of the Boxer Indemnity; the principle of ex-territoriality and foreign control of some of China's sovereign rights; all these and many other matters might be reviewed at this future conference. China wished to be heard there, and the best hope of securing a place at the Council Table seemed to lie in joining the Allies.

China has always been influenced by the United States; she trusts American friendship; and is willing to follow its leadership. The United States is the only great nation which has never deprived China of any of its territorial possessions; by the return of the unused portion of the Boxer Indemnity, she had impressed China with the genuineness of her friendship; through the Chinese students who have gone to America, the best traditions of the Republic had been brought to China. The Chinese Republic was striving after American ideals of freedom and democracy, and in shaping its international policy it was ready to listen to America's voice. Morever, the American Minister at Peking, Dr. Paul S. Reinsch, had a wide influence among Chinese officials.[1] Thus, when the United States severed relations with Germany, China at once followed suit; when America declared war in April, the Chinese leaders were ready to do the same, and were delayed only by the internal situation which at once arose.

In the fourth place, the joining of the Allies seemed to promise to the party in power which made this decision, considerable advantages in strength and prestige, and the Chinese politicians were not slow to grasp this fact.

An example of the reasoning of those in favour of a declaration of war was that of the scholar Liang Chi-chao, whose services to the Republic have already been mentioned.

---

[1] The personal influence of the American Minister and his associates at Peking, throughout all the negotiations leading up finally to a declaration of war, was one of the strongest factors in inducing China to join the Allies.

" The peace of the Far East was broken by the occupation of Kiaochow by Germany. This event marked the first step of the German disregard for international law. In the interests of humanity and for the sake of what China has passed through, she should rise and punish such a country, that dared to disregard international law. Such a reason for war is certainly beyond criticism.

. . . " Some say that China should not declare war on Germany until we have come to a definite understanding with the Entente Allies respecting certain terms. This is indeed a wrong conception of things. We declare war because we want to fight for humanity, international law and against a national enemy. It is not because we are partial towards the Entente or against Germany or Austria. International relations are not commercial connexions. Why then should we talk about exchange of privileges and rights? As to the revision of customs tariff, it has been our aspiration for more than ten years and a foremost diplomatic question, for which we have been looking for a suitable opportunity to negotiate with the foreign Powers. It is our view that the opportunity has come because foreign Powers are now on very friendly terms with China. It is distinctly a separate thing from the declaration of war. Let no one try to confuse the two.

. . . " In conclusion I wish to say that whenever a policy is adopted we should carry out the complete scheme. If we should hesitate in the middle and become afraid to go ahead we will soon find ourselves in an embarrassing position. The Government and Parliament should therefore stir up courage and boldly make the decision and take the step."

Opposed to the four general reasons given for participation on the side of the Allies, there were five groups of arguments. The first was the difficulty China had in reconciling the professed aims of the Allies with its experienced relations with Japan. Rightly or wrongly, for the past twenty years, China had stood in mortal terror of its island neighbour. It had lost to it Formosa, Korea, portions of Manchuria and Mongolia, Tsingtao and the German holdings in Shantung, and had just recently gone through the humiliation of the Twenty-one Demands. The Allied program in Europe called for reparation and restitution for international injuries; China could not understand why this principle should not be accepted in Asia, especially as it applied to its relations with Japan. The existing Terauchi government professed to be friendly to China, but the Chinese felt that such a friendly attitude could not now be reciprocated, unless reparation were made for the acts of the past. Thus fear of Japan was an undoubted obstacle to China's believing in the Allied aims as applied to the Orient.

In the second place, the Chinese were still afraid of Germany's power and feared the eventual vengeance of its army if China should dare to declare war. German propaganda had skilfully magnified German successes and Allied losses, and in 1917 the average Chinese believed firmly that Germany would win the war. German officers had trained the Chinese army, as they had the Japanese troops, and they stood for military efficiency and power in the eyes of the Chinese.

Furthermore, Germany, despite its harsh treatment in the past, had energetically and cleverly conducted a campaign to win the favour of the Chinese, sending out consuls and diplomatic officials who were scholars in Chinese literature and philosophy with sufficient funds to entertain Chinese officials as they like to be entertained; on the other hand, the Allies had at various times, perhaps unconsciously, offended the Chinese. The opium trade,— carried on largely by citizens of the Allied countries in the foreign settlements,— which followed the British " opium war " and the seizure of

Hongkong and other territory; the recent Lao-hsi-kai affair in Tientsin, where French officials attempted to appropriate property which the Chinese thought was theirs; the advice of the American adviser, Dr. Goodnow, to return to the Monarchy; the ineffectual enforcement of the Open Door; all these facts tended to produce a pessimism in the minds of the Chinese regarding idealistic words which seemed to be unbacked by deeds. This pessimism was shared by many of the younger foreign educated leaders in regard to the favourable outcome of the Conference at the close of the war; to many it seemed immaterial whether or not China should have a voice in the council.

In the fourth place, the younger progressive element of the republic feared the new power which would accrue to the more conservative party in control of the government at the time of the war-decision. They were afraid that the new power would be used as Yuan Shih-kai had used the financial support of the five Powers in 1913, to restrict and harm the more democratic tendencies of the Republic.

Other factors were a realization that their own military power was slight, and a fear of "losing face" by comparison with the Allies; the fear that food prices would increase; the devotion to peace, which is deep rooted in the nation; and finally the policy of "proud isolation," which until recent years had marked all China's relations with other nations. It was a long step for a people ruled for centuries by an alien dynasty to attempt republican self-government: it was an almost incredible act for China as a whole to grasp the existing world situation and to take its proper place in relation to it.

An illustration of this general opposition against the declaration of war was the statement of Kang Yu-wei, formerly a fellow-reformer of Liang Chi-chao. In it he said in part:

. . . "The breach between the United States and Germany is no concern of ours. But the Government suddenly severed diplomatic relations with Germany and is now contemplating entry into the war. This is to advance beyond the action of the United States which continues to observe neutrality. And if we analyse the public opinion of the country, we find that all peoples — high and low, well-informed and ignorant — betray great alarm when informed of the rupture and the proposal to declare war on Germany, fearing that such development may cause grave peril to the country.

. . . "Which side will win the war? I shall not attempt to predict here. But it is undoubted that all the arms of Europe — and the industrial and financial strength of the United States and Japan — have proved unavailing against Germany. On the other hand, France has lost her Northern provinces; and Belgium, Serbia and Rumania are blotted off the map. Should Germany be victorious, the whole of Europe — not to speak of a weak country like China — would be in great peril of extinction. Should she be defeated, Germany still can — after the conclusion of peace — send a fleet to war against us. And as the Powers will be afraid of a second world-war, who will come to our aid? Have we not seen the example of Korea? *There is no such thing as an army of righteousness which will come to the assistance of weak nations.* I cannot bear to think of hearing the angry voice of German guns along our coasts!"[1]

Such was the situation in general, following the severance of diplomatic relations with Germany. Public opinion seemed about evenly divided, but nevertheless it seemed fairly certain that the "third step" of the declaration of war against Germany would be taken in due time. Thus, on April 16, following the detention of the Chinese Minister at Berlin, the *Peking Gazette*, the most influential of the papers published by the Chinese, requested an early decision. But at this point the Premier thought fit to summon a council

[1] Putnam-Weale, *The Fight for the Republic in China*, page 334.

of Military Governors and their representatives to hasten the decision of the country, and the ultimate consequences were disastrous.

The conference met April 25. After much arguing and exhorting, the majority of the conference were won over to the view of the Premier. But signs of opposition on the part of the Parliament against the Premier and his supporters began to develop. There was also the feeling that the Premier had promised certain returns from the Allies, such as increase of the Chinese customs duties, and relief from the Boxer indemnity, but that on account of the opposition of Japan, and for other reasons, these returns could not be secured.

On May 1, however, the Cabinet passed the vote for war without asking conditions or returns, and on May 7 the President, through the Cabinet, sent a formal request to Parliament to approve of this declaration. Parliament delayed, and then, on May 10, an attempt was made to force it into a decision by a mob which gathered outside the National Assembly and threatened the members of both houses. There seems to be little doubt that some official of the Government had incited and promised protection to the mob, as it collected at 10 o'clock in the morning, and was not dispersed until 11 at night, when the report was circulated that a Japanese journalist had been killed. The *Peking Gazette* openly accused the Premier of being behind the riot. Telegrams from all parts of the country poured in protesting against this attempted coercing of Parliament; all the Ministers of Tuan's Cabinet resigned, leaving him standing alone.

On May 18, the *Peking Gazette,* edited by Eugene Chen, a Chinese born and educated in England and a British subject, a brave opponent of Yuan Shih-kai and the monarchical schemes, and a staunch supporter of the republic, published an article entitled " Selling China," in which it accused the Premier of being willing to conclude with the Japanese Government an agreement which much resembled Group V of the Twenty-one Demands of 1915. That night Mr. Chen was arrested, and later, without any fair trial, he was sentenced to four months' imprisonment. The case stirred up much comment, and finally, as a result of the intercession of C. T. Wang and others, on June 4, the President pardoned him.

Meanwhile events were marching swiftly. The contest between militants and democrats was clearcut. Demands were made for Tuan's retirement from the Premiership; his military friends on the other hand urged his remaining in office. On May 19, the decision was reached in Parliament that there was a majority for war, but that the question would not be decided while Tuan was Premier. The Military Governors left on May 21 amid much speculation and some fear as to their future action. Before going they sent a petition to the President, indirectly attacking Parliament, by criticizing the Constitution which it had practically finished and asking that Parliament be dissolved if the Constitution were not corrected. The three points to which they objected were:

" 1. When the House of Representatives passes a vote of lack of confidence in the Cabinet Ministers, the President shall either dismiss the Cabinet or dissolve the House of Representatives, but the said House must not be dissolved without the approval of the Senate.   (The French system.)

" 2. The President can appoint the Premier without the countersignature of the Cabinet Ministers.

" 3. Any resolution passed by both houses shall have the same force as law."

Obviously these three points gave more power to the President and to Parliament than an autocratic Premier and his supporters would desire.   The answer to this petition was an increased demand for the retirement of Tuan and the formation of a new Cabinet. The Premier refusing to resign on May 23, the President dismissed him from office.   Wu Ting-fang was appointed acting Premier, and there was a feeling of relief. Li Ching-hsi, nephew of Li Hung-chang, was nominated on May 25 for Premier, and on May 28 his nomination was passed by the House of Representatives, and next day by the Senate. On May 30, C. T. Wang, Chairman of the Committee for Writing the Permanent Constitution, published a statement saying that the second reading was practically finished and reviewing the chief points of interest in the new document ready for promulgation.

The Chinese ship of state seemed to have weathered another of its many storms. But suddenly rumour came from Anhwei that General Ni Shih-chung had declared independence, and that he was backed by Chang Hsun, an unlettered " war lord " of Anhwei, and by most of the other Northern Generals and Governors, who, as Putnam Weale put it, looked upon Parliament and any Constitution it might work out as " damnable Western nonsense, the real, essential, vital, decisive instrument of Government in their eyes being not even a responsible Cabinet, but a camarilla behind that Cabinet which would typify and resume all those older forces in the country belonging to the empire and essentially militaristic and dictatorial in their character." This declaration of revolt was received without approval by the people of the country. The writer talked with men from many sections of the country, and they all agreed that the Military Governors had no definite ideal or purpose, except their own glory and power.

All waited for the President to speak. His answer to this defiance came in no uncertain tones and was received by patriots with enthusiasm. Some of the more important passages in his message were:

" It is a great surprise to me that high provincial officials could have been misled by such rumours into taking arbitrary steps without considering the correctness or otherwise of the same. . . . You accuse the Cabinet of violating law, yet, with the assistance of a military force, you endeavour to disobey the orders of the Government. The only goal such acts can lead to is partition of the country like the five Chi and making the country a protectorate like Korea; in which case both restoration of the monarchy and the establishment of the republic will be an idle dream. You may not care for the black records that will be written against you in history, but you ought certainly to realize your own fate. . . .

" I am an old man. Like the beanstalk under the leaf I have always been watching for any possibility of not seeing and understanding aright. Yea, I walk day and night as if treading on thin ice. I welcome

Copyright by Underwood & Underwood. N. Y.

Feng Kwo-chang, Third President of the Republic, and Staff, in Peking, Oct. 10, 1917.

all for giving me advice and even admonition. If it will benefit the country, I am ready to apologize.

"But if it be your aim to shake the foundations of the country and provoke internal war, I declare that I am not afraid to die for the country. I have passed through the fire of trial and have exhausted my strength and energy from the beginning to the end for the republic. I have nothing to be ashamed of. I will under no circumstance watch my country sink into perdition, still less subject myself to become a slave to another race.

"Of such acts I wash my hands in front of all the elders of the country. These are sincere words from my true heart and will be carried out into deeds.

"LI YUAN-HUNG."

May 31, 1917.

Following the declaration of independence of the northern provinces, most of the southern ones declared their opposition to this stand. They were led by Yunnan, Kweichow, Kwantung, and Kwangsi, who originally opposed the monarchical movement of Yuan Shih-kai in 1916. Some of the loyal Generals' telegrams were hotly worded. From Tang Chi-yao, Governor of Yunnan:

"Chi-yao is unpolished in thoughts and ignorant

of the ways of partisanship or factionism. All he cares and knows about is to protect the republic and be loyal to it. If any one should be daring enough to endanger the Chief Executive or Parliament, I vow I shall not live with him under the same sky. I shall mount my steed the moment order is received from the President to do so."

From a General in Kwantung:

"The reason why the rebels have risen against the Government is that they are fighting for their own posts and for money. That is why their views are so divergent and their acts so ill-balanced. It is hoped the President will be firm to the very last and give no ear either to threat or inducement. This is the time for us to sweep away the remnants of the monarchist curse and reform the administration. With my head leaning against the spear I wait for the order to strike and I will not hesitate even if I should return to my native place a corpse wrapped up in horse-skin!"

The military party nevertheless met at Tientsin and elected Hsu Shih-chang, Generalissimo. But soon signs of dissension appeared among them. On June 7 was made public a friendly warning from America. The American Minister, Dr. Reinsch, transmitted the following message to Dr. Wu Ting-fang, the Minister of Foreign Affairs:

" The Government of the United States learns with the most profound regret of the dissension in China and desires to express the most sincere desire that tranquillity and political co-ordination may be forthwith re-established.

" The entry of China into war with Germany — or the continuance of the status quo of her relations with that Government — are matters of secondary consideration.

" The principal necessity for China is to resume and continue her political entity, to proceed along the road of national development on which she has made such marked progress.

" With the form of government in China, or the personnel which administers that government, the United States has an interest only in so far as its friendship impels it to be of service to China. But in the maintenance by China of one central united and alone responsible government, the United States is deeply interested, and now expresses the very sincere hope that China, in her own interest and in that of the world, will immediately set aside her factional political disputes, and that all parties and persons will work for the re-establishment of a co-ordinate government and the assumption of that place among the powers of the world to which China is so justly entitled, but the full attainment of which is impossible in the midst of internal discord."

This note was welcomed by Chinese as a pledge to support the Central Government. It aroused some resentment in Japan because the Japanese had not been first consulted. On June 9 an ultimatum was sent from Tientsin either by Chang Hsun or by Li Ching-hsi, threatening to attack Peking if Parliament was not dissolved. The President was isolated and members of Parliament and other democrats could not reach him. Rumour reported that he was about to give in and dissolve Parliament. The British adviser to the Chinese Government advised him not to do so. The Japanese adviser gave the opposite counsel. Wu Ting-fang, Acting Premier, refused to sign the mandate. Finally, on June 12, the mandate was issued, countersigned by General Chiang Chao-tsung, commander of the Peking gendarmerie. The next day an explanation was made by President Li in which he admitted he was forced to issue a mandate against his will, but that he did it to save Peking and the country from war and destruction. He declared he would resign as soon as opportunity came.

On June 15, Chang Hsun arrived in Peking with

Li Ching-hsi. Eight of the provinces that week cancelled their independence, stating that their desire for the dissolution of Parliament had been satisfied. The members of the Parliament made their way, many of them in disguise, to Shanghai and there held meetings and sent out manifestoes. Affairs were apparently at a standstill with the country thus divided when the great coup d'état was carried out by Chang Hsun. Affairs thereupon moved swiftly.

On June 30, Kang Yu-wei, a well-known advocate of the monarchy, arrived in Peking. He had travelled incognito from Shanghai. His first visit was to Chang Hsun. On July 1 at 4 A. M. Chang Hsun and his suite called on the Manchu boy-Emperor [1] and informed him of his restoration, and seated him on the throne. President Li Yuan-hung was requested to resign, but refused. He was then practically held prisoner. Numerous imperial edicts were issued, countersigned by " Chang Hsun, member of the Privy Council."

On July 3, Feng Kuo-chang repudiated any connection with the restoration, his name having appeared in the edicts as one of the petitioners. The Military Governor of Canton issued proclamations that the Cantonese would fight to maintain the republic. Many similar messages were sent by other provinces.

[1] Hsuan Tung.

Japanese troops proceeded to the Forbidden City, took President Li Yuan-hung out of the custody of Chang Hsun's men and escorted him to the Japanese Legation. On July 4 the President issued a pledge to support the republic. On July 5 hostilities broke out at Lang Fang on the Peking-Tientsin railway. The diplomatic body notified the Peking authorities that the Procotol of 1901 providing for open railway communication between Shanhaikwan and Peking must be observed. On the same date trains out of Peking were packed to overflowing with Chinese fleeing to Tientsin.

By this time the entire country, with the exception of three provinces, had declared its opposition to the Manchu movement. Tuan Chi-jui came out of his retirement, offering to take command of the Republican army. Liang Chi-chao, who was such a force against Yuan Shih-kai, denounced the whole movement.

The Republican troops advanced upon Peking, and on July 7, American, Japanese, and British soldiers arrived at the capital. An airplane later dropped a bomb over Fengtai station and wrecked the shed. Chang Hsun's troops at Paoma Chang retired inside the capital without fighting and concentrated at the Temple of Heaven. Another airplane flew over the Forbidden City and dropped bombs. Chang Hsun, on

July 8, resigned, but the abdication of the Emperor
was not published, his protector holding out for favourable terms.

Vice-President Feng Kuo-chang assumed the office
of Acting President at Nanking, which was declared
the capital of the Provincial Government. Dr. Wu
Ting-fang arrived in Shanghai with the seal of the
Ministry of Foreign Affairs. Several Ministers of
the Manchu Cabinet on this day were captured while
attempting to escape. Chang Hsun refusing to surrender and 50,000 Republican troops having surrounded
Peking, on July 12, at four in the morning, the attack
was begun in earnest. Several foreigners were
wounded; fire broke out in the Forbidden City; Chang-
Hsun took refuge in the Dutch Legation, and the
Republican flag was raised over the Forbidden City.

On July 14, Tuan Chi-jui arrived in Peking. It is
rather interesting to note that on July 4 practically the
entire country voiced its "declaration of independence" from this Manchu Government; on July 14, the
victorious Republican generals entered the capital.
This opposition and this victory of the Chinese Republicans took place on the Independence Days of the
American and the French Republics; the coincidences
seemed both significant and symbolic. On July 15
Tuan Chi-jui assumed the office of Premier, though

the southern provinces showed opposition to him. On July 17 President Li, in a telegram to the provinces, refused to resume office, and Acting President Feng Kuo-chang expressed his willingness to succeed Li Yuan-hung.

The attitude of liberal Chinese during this crisis was revealed by two speeches made by former officials, July 13, in Shanghai. Dr. Wu Ting-fang, formerly Minister to the United States, who had stood so firmly against any unconstitutional action on the part of the monarchists, said:

" The war in Europe is being fought to put an end to Prussian militarism; and I want the Americans here to understand that China's present troubles are due to exactly the same causes. We are engaged in a struggle between democracy and militarism. Between 55 and 60 per cent. of the taxes of China are now going to support militarism in China. This must be changed, but the change must be gradual. I ask Americans to be patient and give China a chance. Democracy will triumph. Please be patient with us. Study China and try to see us from our own point of view instead of your own.

" I hope to see the day when the Stars and Stripes and fire-coloured flag of China will be intertwined in an everlasting friendship. These nations believe in universal brotherhood; in the rights of the people of small nations to manage their own affairs, as outlined by the great American President in his war declaration. I make this statement with hostility to no nation."

Hon. C. T. Wang, Vice-President of the Chinese Senate, spoke in the same vein:

" The real issues are: Shall there be government by law or by force? Shall the will of the people as expressed through the Assembly prevail, or that of a privileged few? Shall the military forces of the nation be used to uphold the country, or to uphold certain individual generals? Upon these issues the country and the free and democratic nations of the West should be called upon to pass judgment.

" With the strongly ingrained love for democracy and the firm belief in the necessity of subordinating military authority under the civil, in the character of our people, we do not hesitate for a minute to affirm that in China, just as it is in free and democratic nations of the world, constitutionalism shall prevail over militarism. We, like the Entente Allies, have time on our side. We shall have to make the same sacrifices for the final victory of constitutionalism and democracy as they are making in their titanic struggle on the battlefields of Europe.   Let us resolve that we will."

During this period of intense disturbance there was a general feeling among foreigners that assistance should be given to the democratic elements in China in their attempt to defend the Republic.   Especially was American sympathy aroused, and various statements were made by journalists and others, that since America was assisting the newest Asiatic Republic of Russia in its struggle against autocracy, it should also extend its support to the Republicans who were fighting the same battle in China.   Thus Mr. T. F. Millard, a well-known journalist and authority on matters in the Far East, on July 21 voiced his idea of America's duty:

"Yes, it is very inconvenient for democracy, at the time when the issue of a world-war is narrowing down to a test of the fate of democracy, to have two great nations like Russia and China trying republicanism for the first time, and under precarious conditions; for the difficulties of Russia approximate the internal difficulties of China with republicanism.   But just because the local and general conditions are rather unfavourable, and further because of the linking of these experiments with the cause of democracy throughout the world by reason of the war, it becomes virtually impossible for the United States to remain a mere spectator of the course of events in Russia and China. Action to hearten, encourage, and support Russia already has been taken by the United States Government. Action to hearten, encourage, and support China in her effort to maintain a republic ought to be devised and undertaken without delay."

But the Republicans regained control of the government without foreign assistance, and on August 1, Feng Kwo-chang succeeded Li Yuan-hung as President. Before the new President had been in office a week the subject of the declaration of war was again brought up. There was little opposition now to the decision, and on August 14th, 1917, the Chinese Republic formally declared war on the German and Austrian empires.

CHAPTER VI

THE LANSING-ISHII AGREEMENT BETWEEN JAPAN AND AMERICA CONCERNING CHINA

On November 2, 1917, the Lansing-Ishii Agreement between America and Japan was signed at Washington. The agreement, embodied in an exchange of notes, defined the future attitude of these two countries toward China. Its important clauses were two in number: that the United States recognized Japan's " special interests " in China; and that both the United States and Japan repledged themselves to observe the principle of the " open door " and the territorial integrity of China. The agreement was the most important one which had been reached by America in relation to the Orient since the Hay proposal, in 1899, to uphold the principle of the " open door "; and its future bearing on international relations in the Orient will be large.

The general affirmation of the " open door " policy was the remedy proposed by America eighteen years before, to meet the dangerous situation fast developing in China.[1] At that time the prospect of national

[1] The principle of the "open-door," or equal opportunity, in China, was potentially present in Great Britain's first treaty —

disintegration and partition by the world powers seemed imminent. The history of China's relations with the other nations, with the single exception of the United States, was a long story of defeat and losses of Chinese territory and sovereign rights. In 1842, as a result of the victorious "Opium War," Great Britain had taken the Island of Hongkong and, later, portions of the neighbouring mainland; in 1860, Russia acquired Manchurian territory east of the Ussuri River, including Vladivostok and the right to make the city a terminus of the trans-Siberian Railway; in 1864, France had taken Cochin China, and in 1885, proclaimed a protectorate over the nearby territory of Annam and Tongking. A year later, Great Britain conquered and annexed Burma. As a result of the Japanese-Chinese War in 1895, Japan took Formosa and the neighbouring Pescadores Islands; the independence of Korea was recognized, and the Liao-

relations with China in 1842, and the influence of Great Britain in general has been in line with this principle. Anson Burlingame, the first American minister to China, who went out in 1861, was a strong champion of the same ideal. Accordingly the idea was generally current in the Orient long before it was formally recognized in the agreements initiated by Secretary Hay in 1899. The exact phrase, "open-door," was first used in American state-documents in the ultimatum sent to Spain on November 21st, 1898, in reference to the future economic relations with the Philippines.

tung Peninsula, including Port Arthur, was ceded to the Japanese, though Russia, Germany and France at once compelled them to give up the latter territory. Following this war, the spirit of imperialism grew and a scramble for concessions began. As a result of the killing of two missionaries, Germany seized Kiao-chow Bay, including the port of Tsingtao, demanding a ninety-nine year lease, and appropriated the mining and railway rights in Shantung; Russia then requested a similar lease of Port Arthur, and took over practical control of Manchuria; England leased the fortified port of Wei-hai-wei, in Shantung; France gained a port in South China; and Italy asked for, but was refused, territory in Central China along the coast.

Not content with leases, the powers began to stake out "spheres of interest" within which they desired special economic and commercial rights. England's "sphere" was in the Yangtze Valley; Russia's, in the territory north of the Great Wall; France's, in Southwest China; Germany's, in Shantung. If China should be partitioned, these sections would become definite possessions of these nations. The supervision of certain governmental functions of China had already been placed in the hands of citizens of the foreign powers, including the collection of the maritime customs, and later the postal administration and salt-

customs. In the earliest treaty relations, the principle
of "exterritoriality" had been recognized, through
which foreigners were tried by their own laws and
not by the laws of China; later foreign "settlements"
had grown up in various important cities, which were
under complete alien jurisdiction. Following the
marking out of "spheres of interest" came the first
rush for railroad concessions. At this time and within
a few succeeding years, a Franco-Belgian firm, backed
by Russia, acquired the right to build the Peking-
Hankow line; the British, the building of the railway
which joined Shanghai to Nanking and Tientsin, divid-
ing the Shantung rights of the road with the Germans;
American capitalists secured the right of building the
road from Hankow to Canton, but later sold it to the
Chinese government.

This was the situation in China at the end of 1898.
In that year it was to be affected by a policy suggested
by the United States. Up to that time America's foreign policy in the Far East consisted chiefly in an
insistence upon the general principle of non-interference and non-aggression. In 1844, preceding its first
treaty with China, the United States had said: "We
do not desire any portion of the territory of China,
nor any terms and conditions whatever which shall
be otherwise than just and honourable to China as well

as to the United States," and it had lived up to that statement. But, in December, 1898, as a result of the Spanish-American War, the United States was put in possession of the Philippine Islands and there arose at once a need for a formation of a Far Eastern Policy. Great Britain, especially, had begun to look with concern on the situation developing in China and she greeted with cordiality the proposal of Secretary Hay, in 1899, that the principle of the " open door " should be henceforth formally recognized; signifying that thereafter no part of China should be reserved by any nation for its own particular economic or political advantage. This principle was again stated in 1900 in an agreement between Great Britain and Germany and was accepted later by all the Powers, Russia alone making certain reservations. Its important clauses were as follows: first, that no power would in any way " interfere with any treaty port or any vested interest within any so-called ' sphere of interest ' or leased territory which it might have in China "; second, " the Chinese treaty tariff of the time being shall apply to all merchandise landed or shipped to all such ports as are within said ' sphere of interest ' (unless they be ' free ports '), no matter to what nationality it may belong, and . . . duties so leviable shall be collected by the Chinese government "; and, third, "it will levy no higher harbour dues on vessels of another nationality frequenting any port in such 'sphere' than shall be levied on vessels of its own nationality, and no higher railroad charges over lines built, controlled, or operated within its 'sphere' on merchandise belonging to citizens or subjects of other nationalities transported through such 'sphere' than shall be levied on similar merchandise belonging to its own nationals transported over like distances."

In brief, this statement was a pledge by the Powers not to discriminate against each other's business interests in their respective "spheres"; and was a guaranty to maintain the status quo.

The various infringements of Chinese territory and rights, which preceded the formation of this agreement, had naturally had a disturbing effect upon the minds of the inhabitants and the government of China. This found expression in the Boxer outburst in 1900 in which a final attempt was made by force of arms to oust the dreaded foreigner. The attempt was futile and China emerged in 1901, saddled by an indemnity of over $300,000,000, the payment of which was secured by pledges of the customs revenues, the native customs, and a portion of the salt revenues; and with the loss of the liberty to import arms for a limited period, to maintain jurisdiction over the legation quarter in Peking, and certain other national rights. No more territory was given up, however; the "open door" principle was again affirmed; and with certain exceptions in Manchuria, due to the action of Russia, the status quo was maintained until the close of the Russo-Japanese War.

New changes took place at the conclusion of the war between Japan and Russia in 1905, and other alterations in the Far Eastern situation followed, with China again as the victim. By the terms of the Portsmouth Treaty all of Russia's privileges and powers in Southern Manchuria, including Port Arthur and the Russian railways section, were transferred to Japan; Japan's "paramount political, military and economic interests in Korea" were recognized by Russia. Chinese sovereignty in Manchuria was nominally recognized by Russia, but it soon became practically non-existent. In 1910, Korea was formally annexed by Japan. Three years later, as a result of the disturbances of the Republican Revolution, Mongolia becoming temporarily independent, Russia attempted to gain a protectorate over Outer Mongolia, and China was forced to acknowledge Russia's extensive commercial and political privileges there in return for a nominal recognition of its own suzerainty over the region. Japan began to manœuvre in Eastern Inner Mongolia and, in 1915, attempted to clinch its activities by the Twenty-one Demands, in which it affirmed that China had "always recognized its special position in South Manchuria and Eastern Inner Mongolia"; other ambitions were also put forth, as already discussed in another chapter. In Manchuria, further, according to consular reports, Japan had apparently not followed the "open door" agreement of 1899. Such was the changed situation in the China of 1915, as compared to that of 1899. The situation was summarized by Dr. Hornbeck, as follows:

"The settlement at the end of the Russo-Japanese War materially altered the political and geographical alignment. A new status was created. New pledges were made for the maintaining of the newly created status quo. Japan's activities in Manchuria during the next ten years further modified the alignments. In 1914 Japan's conquest of the German possessions in Shantung again abruptly altered the situation. And, finally, Japan's demands upon China in January, 1915, and the granting of the special privileges and concessions which China has been forced to make to Japan constitute a complete upsetting of the balance of power and suggest all the possibilities of a reversion, after the European War shall have been concluded, to speculation, apprehensions, competition, and consequent developments such as marked the years 1895–1898." [1]

This situation, as portrayed, aroused various suspicions of Japan's ultimate intentions toward China, and there seemed a need for some official statement to clear the air. This was made by the Japanese Government in the fall of 1917 in an exchange of notes signed in Washington by Viscount Ishii and Secretary Lansing.

There were three general reasons for the formulation of this agreement. The first was the apprehension of America and of the world in general concerning Japanese intentions in China. These apprehensions were mentioned in the notes exchanged and in a supplementary statement issued by Secretary Lansing. In the notes appears the clause, " In order to silence mischievous reports that have from time to time been circulated, it is believed by us that a public announcement once more of the desires and intentions shared by our two Governments with regard to China is advisable "; and in Secretary Lansing's statement, he said, " There had unquestionably been growing up between the peoples of the two countries a feeling of suspicion as to the motives inducing the activities of the other

[1] *Contemporary Politics in the Far East,* page 242.

in the Far East, a feeling which, if unchecked, promised to develop a serious situation. Rumours and reports of improper intentions were increasing and were more and more believed." German propaganda was referred to as having a large part in increasing this suspicion. This apprehension seemed general not only in America, but in other nations as well, and was one of the reasons for the drawing up of the new agreement.

Another reason, which was not so generally recognized, was Japan's apprehension concerning America's intentions in China. Japan had long cherished the hope of becoming the recognized leader of the Orient. Especially did it desire unquestioned supremacy in its leadership over China. During the past two years the United States had taken certain action which seemed to question its leadership. At the time of the Twenty-one Demands, as already stated, America was the only nation to protest against any infringement of China's rights. In the summer of 1917, during the turmoil which accompanied the attempt to overthrow the Republic and to restore the Manchus, the United States had sent definite advice to China concerning the situation. Statements were made by experienced Japanese journalists, such as, " In the Japanese-American relations, the powder-chest has ever been China — not California "; and that the United States might " go to Japan and tell her that America had taken upon herself the rôle of the guardian and guide of China, that she was to dictate the policy of the Chinese Republic according to what America thought to be just and righteous, and that Japan's policies and actions in the Far East, and more especially in China, were to be subject to the approval of the United States." [1] The formation of the closest possible ties with China seemed vital to the future greatness of Japan, and any interference in such a program was looked upon with apprehension. Accordingly an assurance from America of a continuation of its present relations with China was much desired.

A third factor was the need of the Allies for closer co-operation as a result of the loss of Russia from their ranks. There was a decided need of unity of counsel and of effort, if the handicap of this loss were to be overcome. As has already been pointed out, there had not always been a clear unity of understanding and policy between Japan and the Allies; Japan had special aspirations in the Orient; and there seems reason for the belief that a certain amount of pressure

[1] Adachi Kinnosuke, in *Asia*, December, 1917.

was brought to bear on America to recognize the aspirations of Japan in China. This America apparently attempted to do with justice to China in the Lansing-Ishii Agreement. After a series of conferences in Washington between Viscount Ishii and Secretary Lansing, the following statement was issued on November 2:

" DEPARTMENT OF STATE,
" WASHINGTON, Nov. 2, 1917.
" EXCELLENCY:

" I have the honour to communicate herein my understanding of the agreement reached by us in our recent conversations touching the questions of mutual interest to our Governments relating to the Republic of China.

" In order to silence mischievous reports that have from time to time been circulated, it is believed by us that a public announcement once more of the desires and intentions shared by our two Governments with regard to China is advisable.

" The Governments of the United States and Japan recognize that territorial propinquity creates special relations between countries, and, consequently, the Government of the United States recognizes that

Japan has special interests in China, particularly in the parts to which her possessions are contiguous.

" The territorial sovereignty of China, nevertheless, remains unimpaired, and the Government of the United States has every confidence in the repeated assurances of the Imperial Japanese Government that, while geographical position gives Japan such special interests, they have no desire to discriminate against the trade of other nations or to disregard the commercial rights heretofore granted by China in treaties with other powers.

" The Governments of the United States and Japan deny that they have any purpose to infringe in any way the independence or territorial integrity of China, and they declare, furthermore, that they always adhere to the principle of the so-called ' open door,' or equal opportunity for commerce and industry in China.

" Moreover, they mutually declare that they are opposed to the acquisition by any government of any special right or privileges that would affect the independence or territorial integrity of China, or that would deny to the subjects or citizens of any country the full enjoyment of equal opportunity in the commerce and industry of China.

" I shall be glad to have your Excellency confirm this understanding of the agreement reached by us.

" Accept, Excellency, the renewed assurance of my highest consideration.

" ROBERT LANSING.

" His Excellency, Viscount Ki-
kujiro Ishii, Ambassador
Extraordinary and Plenipotentiary of Japan, on special
mission."

" THE SPECIAL MISSION OF JAPAN,
" WASHINGTON, Nov. 2, 1917.

" Sir:

" I have the honour to acknowledge the receipt of your note today, communicating to me your under-standing of the agreement reached by us in our recent conversations touching the questions of mutual interest to our Governments relating to the Republic of China.

" I am happy to be able to confirm to you, under authorization of my Government, the understanding in questions set forth in the following terms:

(Here the Special Ambassador repeats the language of the agreement as given in Secretary Lansing's note.)

" K. ISHII,

" Ambassador Extraordinary and
Plenipotentiary of Japan, on
special mission.

" Honourable Robert Lansing,
    Secretary of State."

In addition to reaching an agreement on this matter,
the Japanese representatives had also discussed with
the representatives of the United States Government
various other subjects, especially in relation to their
joint participation in the conduct of the war. Secretary Lansing's statement concerning these negotiations was in part:

" The Japanese Commission accomplished a further
purpose in expressing Japan's earnest desire to co-
operate with this country in waging war against the
German government. The discussions covered the
military, naval and economic activities to be employed
with due regard to relative resources and ability. . . .
Complete and satisfactory understandings upon the
matter of naval co-operation in the Pacific have been
reached. . . . At the present time it is inexpedient to
make public the details of these conversations."

The two most important statements in the published agreement were: that both the United States
and Japan repledged themselves to the recognition of
the principle of the " open door " and the territorial
integrity of China; but that the United States also
recognized that Japan had " special interests " in
China, particularly in territory which adjoined its own

Copyright by *Underwood & Underwood, N Y.*

Viscount Ishii, Japanese Ambassador to America, and Reception Committee in New York, 1917. Viscount Ishii is in the centre; Albert H Gary, Chairman of the United States Steel Corporation, is on his left; R. A C Smith, Dock Commissioner and Member of Reception Committee, is on his right.

possessions. It was, indeed, a happy result that China's rights were thus formally recognized and that an assurance was made that the policy of the " open door " was to continue. In this respect the agreement did much to clear away the clouds of suspicion which had been long gathering, and marked a new era in the good relations between the United States and Japan.

On the other hand, there were four main lines of criticism directed against the agreement. In the first place, its terms seemed to be self-contradictory; secondly, the phrase " special interests " was decidedly vague; third, the principle upon which these " special interests " was built, that of territorial propinquity, did not seem to be wholly valid; finally, China was not included in the negotiations.

By reaffirming the principle of the " open door " and of China's territorial integrity, Japan and America seemed to guarantee equal opportunities to all nations in commerce, agreeing also to prohibit any country from acquiring political rights which would infringe China's sovereignty. No commercial or political privileges were to be given to any country. But on the other hand, " special interests " imply special privileges; these privileges must be either commercial or political; and at once a contradiction of meaning seems to arise. The same sort of contradiction had seemed to exist in the treaty between Great Britain and Japan, made in 1905, concerning Korea, when the alliance between the two nations was renewed. Article III of this treaty said, " Japan possessing paramount political, military and economic interests in Korea, Great Britain recognizes the right of Japan to take such measures . . . in Korea as she may deem proper . . . provided that such measures are not contrary to the principle of equal opportunities for the commerce and industry of all nations." [1]   If the phrase " special interests " were substituted for the one " paramount interests," the two affirmations would be more or less similar.   Three months after the treaty between Great Britain and Japan was signed, a Japanese protectorate was established over Korea; five years later Korea was formally annexed.   After the publishing of the Lansing-Ishii treaty with these similar terms there was some fear, especially on the part of China, that history would repeat itself.

In the second place, the phrase " special interests " was obviously vague.   In the agreement they were not defined and there have been various conjectures by the publicists of the three nations involved concerning their meaning.   In a magazine published in Japan shortly after the concluding of the treaty ap-

[1] See Appendix V.

peared two articles which attempted to define these "special interests." The first article maintained that they were special commercial privileges in Japan's various spheres in China; the second insisted that political privileges were designated. In this vagueness of meaning there is possibility of future misunderstanding.

In the third place, the reason for the recognition of these "special interests" was found in Japan's territorial propinquity to China, the principle being stated in the agreement that "territorial propinquity creates special relations between countries" and that consequently Japan was entitled to the "special privileges" named. If China were willing to enter into these special relations with Japan, resulting from the territorial proximity of the two countries, the situation would be different. But any one who has lived in China, whatever his theoretical views may be of the subject, must admit the fact that the Chinese as a whole do not wish to enter into these closer relations with Japan. They are not afraid of loans in which the United States or the other Powers as a group are represented, but they do object to transactions of a commercial or political type with Japan alone. The matter then resolves itself into the question, "Is territorial propinquity a sufficient reason for acquiring special privileges against the will of the people concerned?" The answer in America and in some countries of Europe, in recent years at least, has always been in the negative. Territorial propinquity exists between the United States and Canada; the former desired special relations of reciprocity; but, when Canada did not wish to enter into these relations, there was no question of using force to accomplish them. Germany, on account of its territorial proximity to Belgium and Russia, desires its special commercial relations with them to be recognized, but there is no expectation of this being done. If this principle of self-determination as to special relations, whether commercial or political, applies in America and Europe, why should it not apply in Asia? Further, if territorial propinquity were generally recognized by the other powers as creating special relations, the results might be serious. Russia's boundaries are contiguous with those in China for hundreds of miles; Great Britain could logically claim "special interests" near its port at Hongkong; France could do the same with Cochin China; and America would have a claim in the proximity of the Philippines to the Chinese coast. The Chinese regions implied by reason of their proximity to Japanese possessions would seem to be Manchuria, Mongolia, Shantung, and Fukien; but, if

special interests and privileges were to be conceded in
these provinces and in the regions bordering the holdings of other nations as well, what of the future of
the policy of the " open door " and of equal opportunity, which originally was formulated to check and
control just such spheres of interest?

A fourth objection was that China was not included
in the negotiations. Since the " special interests "
mentioned in the treaty were to be granted to Japan
in China, it would seem that the latter had a right to
a voice in the matter; otherwise its sovereignty seemed
to be ignored. The same action had been taken by
Japan and Russia in the Portsmouth treaty when a
part of the Chinese province of Manchuria was divided
between them and China was not notified until after
the decision concerning the disposal of this territory
had been reached. Although later they ratified this
settlement, the Chinese felt that at that time their rights
as a sovereign nation had not been considered, and the
repetition of this act continued the precedent which
seemed harmful to their national interests and pride.

These were some of the objections made against the
terms of the treaty. Its meaning and influence were
shown more clearly by its reception in each of the three
nations concerned.

As soon as the Chinese government was informed of

the agreement at issue, an official statement "in order to avoid misunderstanding," addressed to both the Japanese and American Governments, was issued. It stated that "the Chinese government had in its relations with foreign governments always followed the principles of justice and equality; that the rights extended to friendly nations by treaty had been consistently respected; that the special relations created by territorial contiguity were provided for in the treaties; and that henceforth as formerly, the Chinese Government would adhere to these principles, but that it could not allow itself to be bound by any agreement entered into by other nations." In other words, China recognized special interests only in so far as they existed by virtue of treaties and agreements to which she was a party.

The Chinese as a whole seemed to appreciate the promises of America and Japan concerning the protection of their territorial rights; but they were in doubt as to the exact meaning of the agreement, due to the double interpretation of the various "special interests." An American authority has characterized it as "a harmless recognition of a simple fact, or a cargo of diplomatic dynamite, according to interpretation and application." He went on to say: [1] "There is no

[1] Article on "The Lansing-Ishii Agreement," in *Asia*, December, 1917. .

question but that for a long time the people of the United States and the people of Japan did not understand the term 'open door' in the same sense. Do they now? Have the American and the Japanese governments achieved a meeting of the minds as to the connotation of the term 'special interests'? In case of disagreement as to whether a given measure does or does not infringe China's independence or the principle of equal opportunity, who is to decide? . . . In 1915 the Japanese Government insisted that its demands upon China did not infringe treaty rights; China insisted that they did. When China, under pressure of an ultimatum, agreed to some fifteen of the things demanded, the United States, without committing itself as to whether they did or did not do so, merely went on record to the effect that it would not recognize any agreement impairing the rights of the United States, the integrity of China, or the principle of the 'open door.'"

Some of the less well-informed Chinese viewed the agreement as a sign of America's tacit approval of Japan's recent action in China. The general attitude seemed to be one of anxiety as to the eventual meaning and implications of the agreement.

Concerning Japan's pledge not to allow any attack upon Chinese territorial integrity, or independence, the

China Press, as quoted in *Millard's Review* of Oct. 6th, said:

"Baron Ishii announces that Japan is 'prepared to defend the independence of China against any aggression.' This is all to the good. There is only one nation that threatens China, and if Japan will defend China against the aggression of that nation, China will survive. If Japan, to put it plainly, will defend China against Japanese aggressions, all will be well."

A final comment was that "no two powers could guarantee between themselves a continuation of China's independence as a sovereign state, or could make certain a preservation of its national territorial integrity. The only way in which these aims could be accomplished seemed to be in a growth of power on China's own part, which would enable it to defend its domains from any aggressions by a foreign power."[1]

The Japanese, although there were some who criticized the agreement because it did not seem definite enough as to their desired powers in China, were generally satisfied with the agreement. The best indication of their approval was the immediate selection of Viscount Ishii as Ambassador to America. They believed that the way was open for their recognized

[1] In the Lansing-Ishii Agreement quoted above.

leadership in the Orient.   One of their publicists, writing in an American magazine, said: " The new understanding between the United States and Japan will be held in Japan as the greatest piece of constructive achievement of the diplomatic history of the Far East for many a generation.   To Japan it is a double triumph. . . . Japan has been the ally of the British Empire for years.   That the greatest power in the two Americas now recognizes her leadership of the Far Eastern states must mean a good deal . . . to my countrymen.   Besides laying a pretty solid foundation stone of the future peace of Japan, the achievement of the Ishii Mission crowns high the cup of Japan's political aspirations." [1]

The view of the treaty taken in the United States, followed a middle course, as compared with these two estimates.   The chief criticism was along the lines already indicated, but America was hopeful that it had solved a difficult situation with satisfaction to both China and Japan.   This attitude was expressed in a statement by Secretary Lansing, accompanying the publication of the treaty.   He said: " By openly proclaiming that the policy of Japan is not one of aggression, and by declaring that there is no intention to take advantage commercially or industrially of the special

[1] Adachi Kinnosuke, in *Asia*, December, 1917.

relations to China created by geographical position, the representatives of Japan have cleared the diplomatic atmosphere of suspicion. . . . The principal result of the negotiations was the mutual understanding which was reached as to the principles governing the policies of the two governments in relation to China. This understanding is formally set forth in the notes exchanged, and now made public. The statements in the notes require no explanation. They not only contain a reaffirmation of the 'open door' policy, but introduce a principle of non-interference with the sovereignty and territorial integrity of China, which, generally applied, is essential to perpetual international peace, as clearly declared by President Wilson, and which is the very foundation, also, of Pan-Americanism, as interpreted by this government."

True friends of China and Japan warmly hope that this estimate of the outcome of the agreement will be borne out by future events.

CHAPTER VII

THE CHINESE-JAPANESE MILITARY AGREEMENT OF 1918

THE situation in Russia following the abdication of the Czar in March, 1917, was of special concern to the Allies. It was of vital importance to the two neighbouring oriental supporters of the Allies, Japan and China. The northern boundaries of the Chinese Republic are contiguous for hundreds of miles with the boundaries of Siberia; any German penetration there would be felt at once in China. Japanese shipping, which included practically all of the vessels on the Pacific, would be menaced at once if the Germans should gain control of Vladivostok. Further, in its larger aspect of German control of Russia's resources and territory, presaging the establishment of a vast empire stretching from the North Sea to the Pacific, the Japanese saw a grave menace. The military danger of the German forces in Siberia seems to have been exaggerated, but there was every probability of economic control and domination. Japan could not take military measures to meet this situation unless it had

the consent and support of its neighbour on the mainland, and consequently, soon after the revolution in
Russia, negotiations were begun leading to a military
agreement between China and Japan. The military
agreement was signed May 16, 1918; the naval agreement, May 19th; the first public announcement was
made in Tokio, May 30th. The whole affair was
shrouded in much secrecy, and was the cause of endless
comment and even suspicion in both countries, which
was not wholly dispelled by the explanatory statement
finally published.

The first report concerning the proposed agreement
became current in China in the Spring of 1917. Unfortunately it was associated in the minds of the Chinese with Group Five of the Twenty-one Demands
made by Japan in January, 1915. These demands
were forecasted by the secret statement of the Black
Dragon Society, already mentioned, which spoke of a
" Defensive Military Alliance " between China and
Japan as the ultimate goal of Japanese foreign policy.
The fifth group of the Demands, it may be remembered, was the most severe, involving certain rights
which, if granted to Japan, would infringe the sovereignty of China and make it practically a vassal
nation.

In its ultimatum of May 7, 1915, Japan, under

threat of force, demanded the acceptance of the first four groups and agreed to hold the fifth group in abeyance, with the exception of the article in relation to Fukien Provinces, saying, " The Japanese Imperial Government will undertake to detach the Group Five from the present negotiations and discuss it separately in the future." Commenting on this clause, a leading journalist in the Orient, Mr. Putnam-Weale, had said, " It is this fact which remains the sword of Damocles hanging over China's head; and until this sword has been flung back into the waters of the Yellow Sea the Far-Eastern situation will remain perilous." [1] The Twenty-one Demands were prefaced by the statement that they were being made for the purpose " of maintaining the general peace in Eastern Asia," and it was not surprising that, when Japan began negotiations for a military alliance, having a similar purpose, last year, many Chinese began to fear that the long-dreaded " sword of Damocles " was about to fall.

The first specific mention of the proposed alliance was made in the *Peking Gazette,* the most influential native newspaper, on May 18, 1917. The editor, Eugene Chen, who has already been mentioned, was a fiery supporter of the Republic and an opponent of the Japanese. In an editorial entitled " Selling China,"

[1] *The Fight for the Republic in China,* page 117.

he asserted that the Premier, Tuan Chi-jui, was contemplating making an agreement with Japan which would involve practically all the concessions mentioned in the original Group Five. Mr. Chen was promptly arrested and thrown into prison without a trial; later his newspaper was suppressed and its property confiscated. Subsequently Mr. Chen was pardoned and made his escape from Peking; but his accusation lingered in the minds of the Chinese public and became associated with any mention of a military alliance with Japan.

Matters remained at a standstill until the early months of the year 1918, when reports again began to circulate, saying that the agreement was soon to be made. The wildest and most extravagant stories became current. The statement was freely made that the northern officials were selling China for their own interests. In March it was recorded that a preliminary agreement had been signed, and protests from all the country were sent to Peking.

An example of these rumours was a letter published in the *China Press* in April. It was written by a Chinese who claimed to have gained his information directly from one of the high officials in Peking. The *China Press* published it with the following comments:

" The *China Press* some weeks ago received from its Peking correspondent word that new demands or ' requirements' had been presented by Japan. Since then Reuter's Agency has also carried the reports. In the light of those facts, the following letter, although its authority cannot be vouched for, is interesting:

" ' I hope you have perused my last letter. Since then there has been another exceedingly alarming occurrence. This is in connection with the revival of the negotiations with a certain country to form a certain alliance for participation in the great war. Its inside facts are as follows:

" ' (1)   Warfare alliance, including the training of soldiers under their supervision.

" ' (2)   Arms alliance, including the organization of arsenals with joint Chinese and — interest.

" ' (3)   Industrial alliance, including the practical surrender of all the mines of the republic.

" ' (4)   Financial alliance, including a loan to China amounting to $60,000,000, the control of the issue of banknotes and the reorganization of the banks of China and communications.

" ' (5)   Educational alliance.

" ' (6)   Diplomatic alliance.

" ' (7)   Transportation alliance.'

" This is certainly more alarming than Group Five

of the Twenty-one Demands presented in the fourth year of the Republic. Another demand included in the present negotiations is that China shall not sign any treaty or agreement with any foreign power without the consent of the government in question.

"This new pact went into force on May 1. It is learned that it was officially signed and sealed. The special mission of the Minister of the nation concerned was solely for the purpose of effecting the conclusion of the alliance.

"Although it appears on the surface as a document of an alliance for participation in the war, it really amounts to a bill of sale of the nation. This is a continuation of what was intended to be effected in the fourth year of the republic, only it has been immensely enlarged upon and is a hundred times more detrimental.

"This piece of news is obtained through Chow Tse-chi from the 'Money Joss.' (Liang Shih-yi.)"

Finally, on May 16th, an official statement from both Peking and Tokyo was published, stating that an agreement had been reached. The fears of the Chinese were heightened by the fact that the officials would not publish the terms of the alliance. Similar secrecy had surrounded the serving of the Twenty-one Demands in 1915, and many alarmists recalled this fact. The editor of the chief native newspaper in Peking committed suicide, saying that he would not live to become a slave of a foreign country. The Chinese students in Japan attacked the Chinese embassy in Tokyo and then left in a body for China. The leaders of the Southern party in China telegraphed Peking that they would give up their opposition to the Central Government if it would cancel the agreement. Even in Japan there was much adverse criticism of the secrecy maintained by the Imperial Government. Finally this feeling grew so strong that on May 30th an official statement was made concerning the agreement. It took the form of a denial of the many rumours which had arisen, rather than a clear exposition of the agreement itself. It mentioned certain notes which had been exchanged on March 25th between the Japanese Minister of Foreign Affairs and the Chinese Minister in Tokyo. These notes were of the greatest importance, as they stated that the military agreement had relation only to the hostile penetration into Russian territory, and the assurance was given that Japanese troops, stationed within Chinese territory for the purpose of defence, would be completely withdrawn upon the termination of the war. The period within which the notes were to remain in force was to be determined by the military and naval authorities of the two powers. The notes follow:

Mr. Chang to Viscount Motono

"Tokyo, March 25, 1918.— I have the honour to communicate to Your Excellency that the Government of China, believing that in the present situation co-operation with the Government of Japan on the lines hereinafter indicated is highly important in the interest of both countries, have authorized me to approach your Government with a view to arranging for such co-operation.

" 1. Having regard to the steady penetration of hostile influence into Russian territory, threatening the general peace and security of the Far East, the Government of China and the Government of Japan shall promptly consider in common the measures to be taken in order to meet the exigencies of the situation, and to do their share in the Allied cause for the prosecution of the present war.

" 2. The methods and conditions of such co-operation between the Chinese and Japanese armed forces in the joint defensive movements against the enemy for giving effect to the decision which may be arrived at by the two Governments in common accord under the

Copyright by Underwood & Underwood, N. Y.

Review at Peking of Chinese Troops, a Detachment of whom have Joined the Allied Forces in Siberia
The influence of German military training in the Orient is shown by the fact that Chinese soldiers, like the Japanese, adopt the goose-step in review.

preceding clause, shall be arranged by the competent authorities of the two powers who will from time to time consult each other fully and freely upon all questions of mutual interest. It is understood that the matters thus arranged by the competent authorities shall be confirmed by the two Governments and shall be put into operation at such time as may be deemed opportune."

Viscount Motono replied on the same day with an identic note recapitulating Mr. Chang's statements and adding:

" The Imperial Government, fully sharing the views embodied in the foregoing proposals, will be happy to co-operate with the Chinese Government on the lines above indicated."

Viscount Motono to Mr. Chang

" Tokyo, March 25, 1918.— With reference to the notes exchanged on March 25 between the Governments of Japan and of China on the subject of their joint defensive movements against the enemy, I have the honour to propose on behalf of my Government that the period within which the said notes are to remain in force shall be determined by the competent military and naval authorities of the two Powers. At the same time the Imperial government are happy to declare that the Japanese troops stationed within Chinese territory for the purpose of such defensive movements against the enemy shall be completely withdrawn from such territory upon the termination of the war."

Mr. Chang to Viscount Motono

" Tokyo, March 25, 1918.— I have the honour to acknowledge the receipt of Your Excellency's communication under today's date, proposing on behalf of your Government that the period within which the said notes are to remain in force shall be determined by the competent military and naval authorities of the two Powers. I am happy to state in reply that the foregoing proposal is accepted by my Government. I am further gratified to take note of the declaration embodied in your communication under acknowledgment, that the Japanese troops stationed within Chinese territory for the purpose of defensive movements against the enemy shall be completely withdrawn from such territory upon the termination of the war."

These notes were apparently the foundation of the reports current during the last of March in China, although there is evidence for the view that the first demands of the Japanese were more extreme than these notes indicate. In addition to these notes the

Japanese government issued a supplementary statement categorically denying all such interpretations of
the agreement. The statement follows:

" Having regard for the steady penetration of hostile influence into Russian territory, jeopardizing the
peace and welfare of the Far East, and recognizing
the imperative necessity of adequate co-operation between Japan and China to meet the exigencies of the
case, the Governments of the two countries, after
frank interchange of views, caused the annexed notes
to be exchanged, March 25, between the Minister of
Foreign Affairs and the Chinese Minister in Tokyo.

" In pursuance of the purport of the notes the Imperial Government subsequently sent Commissioners
representing the Imperial Army and Navy to Peking,
where they held conferences with the authorities of the
Chinese army and navy. The negotiations progress-
ing smoothly, two agreements were concluded, one relating to the army being signed May 16, and the other
relating to the navy, May 19.

" These agreements only embody concrete arrangements as to the manner and conditions under which
the armies and navies of the two countries are to co-
operate in common defence against the enemy, on the
basis of the above mentioned notes exchanged on
March 25. The details of the arrangements consti-

tuting as they do a military secret, can not be made public, but they contain no provision other than those pertaining to the object already defined. Currency has been given to various rumours, alleging that the agreements contain for instance such stipulations as that a Chinese Expedition is to be under Japanese command, that Japan may construct forts in Chinese territory at such places as she may choose, that Japan will assume the control of Chinese railways, shipyards, and arsenals, and even that Japan will assume the control of China's finances, will organize China's police system, will acquire the right of freely operating Chinese mines producing materials for the use of the arsenals, etc. It cannot be too emphatically stated that these and similar rumours are absolutely unfounded.

" May 30, the 7th year of Taisho,
    " Ministry of Foreign Affairs,
        " Tokyo, Japan."

In this statement there is no definite information given concerning the details of the arrangement. Considerable speculation has taken place in regard to these details. President Feng was rumoured to have shown them to a delegation of students who came to him to protest against the agreement. Various versions have been published unofficially; a translation of

CHINESE-JAPANESE MILITARY AGREEMENT 139

one of them which comes from semi-official sources, read as follows:

" Article 1. In view of the penetration of enemy influence into the eastern territory of Russia, and of the likelihood of the peace of the two contracting parties being disturbed thereby, China and Japan mutually agree actively to undertake the obligations of war-participation by measures designed jointly to guard against the action of the enemy.

" Article 2. The two countries shall mutually recognize and respect the equality of the other regarding position and interests in carrying out joint military measures.

" Article 3. When it is necessary to take action based on this agreement, orders will be issued by both China and Japan to their troops and people, calling on them to be frankly sincere in dealing with each other in the area of military operations; and the Chinese officials shall co-operate and assist the Japanese troops in the area involved so that there may be no hindrance to military movements. Japanese troops shall on their part respect Chinese sovereignty and shall not cause any inconvenience to the Chinese people by violating local customs and traditions.

" Article 4. Japanese troops in Chinese territory shall withdraw from China as soon as war is ended.

"Article 5. If it be found necessary to send troops outside of Chinese territory, troops will be jointly sent by the two countries.

"Article 6. The war area and war responsibilities shall be fixed by mutual arrangement of the military authorities of the two countries as and when occasion arises in accordance with their respective military resources.

"Article 7. In the interests of convenience, the military authorities of the two countries shall undertake the following affairs during the period necessary for the execution of joint measures: —

"1. The two countries shall mutually assist and facilitate each other in extending the means of communications (post and telegraph) in connection with military movements and transportation.

"2. When necessary for war purposes construction operations may be carried on and the same shall be decided, when occasion arises, by mutual consent of the chief commanders of the two countries. The said construction-operation shall be removed when the war is ended.

"3. The two countries shall mutually supply each other with military supplies and raw materials for the purpose of jointly guarding against the enemy. The quantity to be supplied shall be limited to the extent

Japanese Troops, in Allied Expeditionary Force in Siberia.

Half of this force is composed of troops from Japan; General K. Otani is the Commander-in-Chief.

of not interfering with the necessary requirements of the country supplying the same.

" 4. Regarding questions of military sanitation in the war area the two countries shall render mutual assistance to each other.

" 5. Officers directly concerned with war operations shall .mutually be sent by the two countries for co-operation. If one party should ask for the assistance of technical experts, the other shall supply the same.

" 6. For convenience, military maps of the area of war operations will be exchanged.

" Article 8. When the Chinese Eastern Railway is used for military transportation, the provisions of the original treaty relating to the management and protection of the said line shall be respected. The method of transportation shall be decided as occasion arises.

" Article 9. Details regarding the actual performance of this agreement shall be discussed by mutual agreement of the delegates appointed by the Military Authorities of the two countries concerned.

" Article 10. Neither of the two countries shall disclose the contents of the agreement and its appendix, and the same shall be treated as military secrets.

" Article 11. This Agreement shall become valid when it is approved by both Governments after being signed by the Military representatives of the two countries. As to the proper moment for the beginning of war operations, the same shall be decided by the highest military organs of the two countries. The provisions of this agreement and the detailed steps arising therefrom shall become null and void on the day the joint war measures against the enemy end.

" Article 12. Two copies of the Chinese and of the Japanese text of this agreement shall be drawn; one of each shall be kept by China and Japan. The Chinese and Japanese texts shall be identical in meaning." [1]

The main feeling in the Orient concerning the alliance was one of relief and of surprise at the long period of secrecy that shrouded the negotiations — a secrecy which tended to increase any misunderstanding which might have arisen. A general explanation of this secrecy by Japanese, as well as Chinese writers, was that Japan attempted to gain more than was contained in the final agreement; that her original plan had to be modified by the counter-proposals of the Peking Government. There was also a tendency to criticize the statement for not being more explicit. Thus, according to the *Japan Advertiser* of May 31st, " Mr. Yuko Hamuguchi, a prominent member of the Kenseikai, remarks that the agreement has caused misunderstanding and much excitement among many Chinese, and though an official statement has now been published the agreement will remain as much a conundrum as ever, inasmuch as the important clauses are kept secret. It seems problematical whether the official statement just published will have the desired effect in removing the suspicion of the Chinese."

On the other hand, there was a general appreciation of the promises of Japan to retire when the military necessity permits, and a feeling that, because of the alliance, Japan and China were the better prepared to do their part in the final phases of the great war. Thus the *Japan Advertiser* commented editorially upon the alliance; its views were seconded by the hopeful-minded press of the Orient. " The categorical denial of the rumours so widely current in China is a conclusive reply to the sensation-mongers who have been so active. The present emphatic disclaimer will have great value in restoring China's confidence in Japan, and may mark a turning point in the relations of the two countries. That may be counted positive gain, in addition to the confounding of malicious rumours. The other positive gain is that the way is clear for whatever action may be called for by further enemy penetration of Russian territory. . . . There is ample justification for the agreement, and the Allies will sincerely rejoice that the way is clear for action, if action should be necessary."

Since these words were written an Allied force has entered Siberia. After a wise and prolonged deliberation, the United States government decided to send a military force to join with troops from Japan and China and others of the Allied nations, in the attempt to strengthen the Czecho-Slovaks in their revolt against the Bolsheviks and the Germans in Russia.[1] Solemn assurances have been made to the people of Russia, that this Allied force has no intention of infringing any of the nation's rights, but that its presence is merely a guarantee of Allied support in the attempt of Russia to free itself from the invader and the traitor. The ranking officer in the expeditionary force of the Allies is the Japanese General, K. Otani; Chinese troops are co-operating under his command; and from elsewhere along the frontier, reports have come of other Chinese soldiers having repulsed forces of the Red Guards. Thus, China is realizing its ambition of assisting in a military way, as well as industrially, in the world-war for international justice and freedom.

[1] Note: The Allied Force numbered about 24,000 in the summer of 1918. Of this number half were Japanese and the balance was composed of American, Chinese, British, French and Italian soldiers.

CHAPTER VIII

THE FUTURE OF CHINA AS AFFECTED BY THE AIMS OF THE ALLIES

WHEN the American Republic joined the Allies in the Great War, President Wilson summarized its ideal and purpose in so doing, by the sentence: " The World must be made safe for Democracy." The Allied Nations have generally accepted this expression of their ideal and purpose. When President Wilson's words were cabled to the Orient they produced a profound impression there. At once observers pointed out that the President had not limited the application of this ideal to Europe or to America alone, but that it was all-inclusive and was to apply to Asia as well. At once came a realization of the greatness of the ideal and of its possibilities as a solution for the problems of the Orient. Further, the view was widely expressed that these Asiatic problems must be solved if the cause of the Allies was to be permanently successful.

Many considerations seemed to point to that conclusion. This is a world-war and nothing less than a world-peace would seem to be adequate. From this world-peace, Asia cannot be excluded. Half of the world's population is in Asia; in India, Asiatic Russia, in China, and Japan. China is the largest and oldest nation in the world; its future cannot be ignored. A recent writer [1] has pointed out that after the war there will be three great groups of world-races: the Anglo-Saxons, the Slavs and the Mongolians. The first group has far outdistanced the other two in political development and progress; it has bravely taken the stand that its ideals of democracy and liberty shall be permitted to become world-wide. In the Orient, the Chinese people have thrown off the restraints of an alien autocratic dynasty, and are groping unsteadily towards the light of democracy in the form of a republic. Russia has only recently taken a similar step; in both lands there is confusion and disorder; but both peoples are on the right road, and if given time and sympathetic support, they will reach their goal. America and the Allied nations have expressed their faith in Russia, and have pledged themselves to stand by her; they will certainly do no less for China. In Japan, as well, liberal tendencies are appearing; the country is at the cross-roads of its history; on the one hand, facing an imperialistic course that cannot but mean danger, and aggression upon its neighbours; on

[1] William S. Howe, *Asia*, July 18, 1918.

the other hand, halting before the decision to align itself with the international tendencies of the age in a fair and friendly national policy toward all the world. These aspirations and tendencies in Asia must be considered in the Peace Conference. The writer makes bold to say that unless this is done, the consequences from the standpoint of a maintenance of the world-peace will be disastrous.

Before the great war two political storm-centres were recognized in the world: the Balkans in the Near East and China in the Far East.[1] In both " legitimate interests " of the various nations clashed and this clash in Europe was the immediate occasion of the outbreak of the great war. It is hoped that the Allied peace terms will permanently remove the causes of future conflict in the Balkans at the close of the war; they should aim at no less satisfactory a solution of the problems in China.

A future outbreak in the Far East might come in one of two ways: either as a result of international friction in China; or through a war between China and Japan which would involve the other powers. The story of the growth of the competitive spheres of inter-

---

[1] " China will become, through the jealousy and the indifference of the Western Powers, the most dangerous storm-centre in the world after a European peace is concluded." F. W. Williams, *The Nation*, November 22, 1917.

est in China; the attempted check to their rivalry and enforcement of the status quo by an agreement as to the principle of the "open door" and equal opportunity; the upsetting of this situation by encroachments of Russia and Japan; has already been told. At the close of the great war there will be a renewed competition for China's trade and control of her natural resources and the means of transportation and production. Japan has tried to forestall the other powers by its action in the Twenty-one Demands and the Chengchiatung affair. Japanese and British interests as a result definitely clash. Russia, France and Belgium are also involved. If no clearly recognized principle of justice and equity is to be enforced, there seems grave probability of the growth of friction and dissension which may lead to future armed conflict.

The second line which future hostilities might take would be in a clash between China and Japan which would eventually involve the other nations. The lack of friendship and mutual trust between the Chinese and the Japanese is a disturbing factor in the Orient. These feelings of ill-will and distrust have been the outgrowth of a lack of justice and fair play in their relations with each other. At present Japan has the ascendancy, and China is no match for her in military power or national strength; but if China goes forward in development, as it would seem she must, an armed struggle in the future seems inevitable. Russia and Great Britain are both involved in defensive alliances with Japan, but they, as well as all the other great nations, have relations with and interests in China, and it would seem they might eventually be dragged into such a conflict.

Such possibilities are not pleasant to contemplate; the common-sense view would seem to be, not to ignore them, but to take action at the close of the war, to prevent their development. The solution would seem to lie along the line taken in the adjusting of the international difficulties of Europe.

With the principles of this adjustment, China is in sympathy and although hampered by internal difficulties, she has made what contributions she could to the Allied cause. When the war broke out, Germany's commercial interests were strongly entrenched throughout China; Germany's trade was increasing rapidly; German interests were being aggressively and successfully pushed. An effort had been made to secure the adoption in the higher schools of China, of German as the only foreign language to be taught there; and this effort very nearly succeeded. Germany had seized and fortified an important military and naval base on the Chinese coast; by a widespread campaign of propaganda, German victories in the war were magnified and Germany's future importance was impressed upon the Chinese. As a result, during the first two years of the war, the Chinese were, in general, mildly pro-German. The change of sentiment expressed by the severance of diplomatic relations and the declaration of war, was great indeed, and already has had important effects in frustrating Germany's hope of dominance in the Far East. German and Austrian property and banks have been taken into custody and their ships turned over to the Allies; German and Austrian subjects have been registered and interned. In the summer of 1918, arrangements were made in compliance with the request of Great Britain and her Allies to transport all enemy aliens to Australia. This step aroused such violent threats of reprisals by Germany that the Allies, led by Japan and Great Britain, requested China not to carry it out. The desire of Germany to keep her nationals in China, reveals her estimate of the importance of her interests there, and it is no small thing from the standpoint of the future power of Germany, that these interests have been virtually rendered non-existent.[1]

In the second place, China has sent large forces of

[1] The Allies in October made a joint statement requesting more stringent control over German activities in China.

labour battalions to France to carry on work behind the lines and thus relieve soldiers for the front. They number about one hundred and seventy-five thousand and they have performed very efficient service.[1]

In a military way, Chinese troops are co-operating with the Allied force which has entered Siberia and will help to safeguard the long boundaries stretching from the coast into inner Russia.

Finally, China is one of the great storehouses of the world's food supply; large shipments of rice and eggs and other staples have been made to the Allies, and these shipments will increase as the war continues.

On August 19th, announcement was made that the Chinese Government had received a thirty million dollar contract for building ships for the Allies in the shipyards at Shanghai.

Concerning China's future contribution to the Allies, if a prolongation of the war should make this necessary, Dr. V. K. Wellington Koo, the Chinese Minister, speaking on Oct. 1st, China Day of the fourth Liberty Loan Campaign, in New York, said as follows:

" It is practical to say that with a fair supply of

[1] The distribution of these labour-battalions, according to a report received at the Chinese Legation in Washington, in October, 1918, was as follows: With the British forces, 125,000; with the French, 40,000; with the Americans, 6,000; in Mesopotamia and Africa, about 4,000. Total, 175,000.

equipment in ships, not only labour battalions, but fighting soldiers, not only thousands of them but millions of them, can be dispatched to Europe. It is equally practical to say that with a fair amount of capital the natural resources of China, the resources of coal and iron, of copper and zinc, of antimony and tungsten — all essential articles of war,— can be developed and utilized to untold advantage. Even production of foodstuffs can be so increased as to make China the world's great granary for the sustenance of the Entente troops."

After China entered the war, the Allies granted a temporary suspension of the payment of the Boxer Indemnity and an increase in the tariff rates to an effective 5 per cent. But the Chinese feel that the only ultimate solution for their national difficulties is a recognition by the other powers of their rights as a sovereign nation, with all that this implies in the coming world-situation. Their deepest hope is that the principles for which the Allies are fighting will be applied to the Orient. Thus a prominent Chinese lawyer and scholar, Dr. M. T. Z. Tyau, in 1917, expressed the national attitude:

" For the great powers to welcome China into their charmed circle in one breath and in the next, deny her what are her proper attributes and prerogatives as an independent sovereign state is ingenious and disingenuous. The status of membership in the Family of Nations having been acknowledged, it is but just that all her sovereign rights should be completely restored to her. Unless this is done, it seems that this terrible war will have been fought in vain. We are, however, not despondent and we remain confident that at the post-bellum peace conference full justice will be done to her rightful claims, because out of this ordeal of fire there will evolve a world in which, as Lord Grey said on March 22, 1915, all nations will be ' free to live their independent lives, working out their form of government for themselves, and their own national development, whether they be great nations or small states — in full liberty.' "

Dr. Koo, the Chinese minister to the United States, in an address in New York last year, expressed the national hope of the present time, and paid a tribute to the example America had set in its relations to China which might be prophetic of future relations with the world at large. He said:

" In the first place, the people of the Far East feel that in any reconstruction which may take place after the war, the Far East should be included; that the problems of the Far East should receive due consideration. . . . In the second place, the reflective minds of the Far East feel that not only the problems of the Far East should be given full consideration, but also the voices of the Far East should be freely heard at the council board of nations. . . . There is, in the third place, yet another thought which is quickening the hearts of a very large portion of the people in the Far East, particularly of the people in China, and that is, that in any reconstruction to take place hereafter, the base of the foundation should be built upon justice,— international justice. The people of the Far East in general feel that every act of aggression, wherever arising, should be a matter of concern, not only of the victim and oppressed, but should also be of serious interest to the world at large; for every act of aggression or oppression, unchecked and uncondemned, is sure to react to the detriment of the international society.

" Here between China and the United States, for instance, we have a concrete example of how two nations, always basing their mutual intercourse on justice, could get along in cordial relationship and in perfect understanding; more than a century of trade intercourse, eighty-seven years of missionary work, seven decades of diplomatic relations and nearly half a century of educational co-operation, have all been characterized by a sustained feeling of friendliness and cordiality, so that Chinese and Americans, wherever they meet, can always talk to each other without hidden thoughts and with perfect confidence in the good will of each toward the other. There is no suspicion or friction between them. The two countries are living in a happy state of friendship that grows from day to day. What two countries have done can be accomplished by the world at large." [1]

The problems which China will face at the end of the war will be many and various. Most of them come as a result of the attempts to adjust a civilization and political organization, which have come down practically unchanged from past centuries, to the new national and international life of the twentieth century. Three problems especially are serious: those related to the political, the economic, and the educational conditions of the country.

The development of the Republic since 1911 has already been treated in some detail. At present (October, 1918) the country is divided into a progressive South with headquarters at Canton; a conservative North with Peking as its capital; and a more or less neutral centre situated along the Yangtze Valley, with Nanking as its chief city. Until September the administration was in the control of the Northerners

[1] *Current History Magazine,* November, 1917.

and the neutrals, with Tuan Chi-jui, as Premier, representing the first group, and Feng Kwo-chang, from Nanking, as President, representing the second. On September 4th, Hsu Shih-chang, a representative of the Northern party, was elected President to succeed Feng Kwo-chang, by a Parliament which was convened on August 12th in Peking. The South has protested against the Parliament and the election and on October 6th formally declared its opposition to the President.

The development of this unsatisfactory situation followed the dissolution of Parliament, on June 12th, 1917. Later a national council was organized by the Northerners which revised and passed laws for a new parliamentary organization and election. These new laws were promulgated in February, 1918, and elections were held in the spring and summer. On August 12th, the new parliament was convened at Peking. The membership of the former assembly had been 870; that of the new one was reduced to 573 (274 Senators and 405 representatives). It was composed largely of former officials and their friends and relatives, although there was a sprinkling of returned students. The two speakers elected, Liang Shih-yi of the Senate, and Wang Yih-tang of the House, had both held important positions under Yuan Shih-kai; the former as his chief Secretary and Acting Minister of Finance; and the latter as military adviser and military governor of Kirin. Liang especially was associated with the movement to restore the Monarchy. On September 4th, in accordance with the new election law, Parliament elected a president to succeed Feng Kwo-chang, who had followed Li Yuan-hung, who in turn had taken office at the death of Yuan Shih-kai. The new President's term of office began October 10th, when the first presidential term dating from 1913 was held legally to have expired. Five provinces of the south and southwest abstained from any participation in the preceding events, as has already been indicated.

The new president has held various positions of importance under the Manchus, being Viceroy of Manchuria in 1907, President of the Privy Council under Prince Ching, and one of the two guardians of the Boy Emperor. He was Secretary of State of the Republic under Yuan Shih-kai in 1915, and was a close friend, being called one of the four " sworn brothers," of Yuan. At the time of his election to the presidency he did not hold an official position, and although he was the candidate of the military party, he was not a military leader; so it was hoped he would prove acceptable to the Southern Republicans. After his election he sent out a circular telegram calling on all those with administrative experience to come forward to assist in solving the difficulties confronting the country, the chief of which he enumerated as the unfinished state of the constitution, the emptiness of the treasury, internal strife and brigandage, and the certainty that after the European war, China would be the centre of a vigorous commercial contest.

The hope that the new President would command the support of the South has not been realized and the South is ranged solidly against him. Ever since the dissolution of the National Assembly, and the coup d'état of Chang Hsun in July, 1917, the South has been in a state of revolt, its two chief demands being the reconvening of the dissolved Parliament and the return to the Provisional Constitution until a permanent one can be finally drafted. Among the Southern leaders are some of the ablest Chinese. The Administrative Council includes Sun Yat-sen, the first Provisional President of the Republic; Wu Ting-fang, former Minister to America; Tang Shao-yi, former Premier; Lu Yung-ting, formerly military Governor of Kwangtung; and Tsen Chun-hsuan, President of the Board of Communications. Members of the former Parliament had gathered at Canton and on August 8th both houses had a quorum and set about completing the permanent

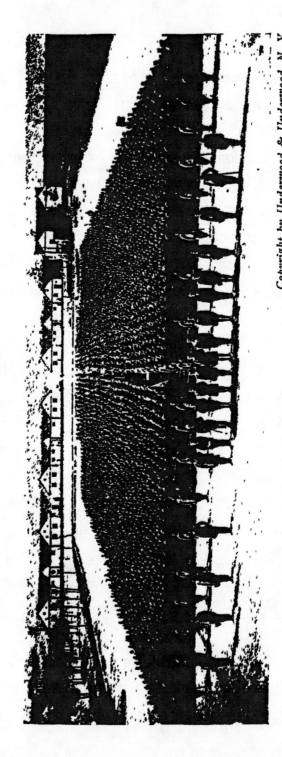

Chinese Labor Battalions Ready for Embarkation to France.

175,000 Chinese have been sent to France for work behind the lines. This detachment started from Tsingtao, formerly a German stronghold in China.

Constitution, and drafting new election and parliamentary-organization laws. C. T. Wang, formerly vice-president of the Senate, and chairman of the committee for drafting the permanent constitution, which had practically finished its work before the dissolution of Parliament in June, 1917, is acting chairman of the new Senate.

Aside from this direct issue between the North and the South, the chief menace to a national unity has been the independent control of the various provincial governors over large bodies of troops who are loyal to them rather than to the central government, and through whose support the governors can carry out individual policies regardless of their effect upon the welfare of the nation as a whole. The leaders in the Northern Government have also adopted a reckless course of borrowing capital from Japan in order to gain support for their military operations against the South. As security, they have apparently mortgaged some of China's native resources. Further, their recent attempt to revive the opium trade has called forth a protest from the United States and Great Britain.[1] But despite these deficiencies and dissensions, there are

[1] On November 20th the announcement was made in Peking that the government had purchased and would destroy the entire stock of opium remaining in China.

grounds for hope for the future. The Chinese have shown themselves much more restrained than the Russians in their attempt to set up a democracy and should gradually achieve national unity and efficiency, even though allied mediation and assistance may become a temporary necessity to this end.

Economically, China is in a low stage of development. She has not passed from the agricultural and commercial levels to the industrial and manufacturing stages, and poverty is general and oppressive. The standards of sanitation and public health are among the lowest in the world. There is a decided lack of means of transportation by road or by rail. There is no exact system of coinage, and the country is on a silver basis, and is subject to its many fluctuations.[1] The governmental resources, such as the maritime tariff and the salt customs, are under the control of foreigners, and cannot be increased without their consent. Further, the payment of the Boxer indemnity has taken much of these revenues. The only course open to the government has been to borrow, and this action has saddled upon it heavy foreign debts. With these loans has often come control over rights within the country. Since the beginning of the war, Japan alone has loaned

[1] A hastily-devised scheme to change to a gold standard similar to that of Japan, which was announced Aug. 10th, 1917, was greeted with protests by the international interests concerned.

to China over $100,000,000,[1] thereby, in the view of the Chinese, increasing its hold on the country. On the other hand, when compared to the enormous war debts which the other nations will face at the close of the present struggle, China will be comparatively well off, its total foreign debt in 1917, exclusive of railroad debt, being about $750,000,000,[2] or less than $2.00 per capita. Already attempts are being made to improve the hygienic condition of the cities, and to build up modern industries. Commerce is growing rapidly.[3] The Allies have granted a temporary suspension of the Boxer indemnity and an increase in the tariff; and a four-power group, consisting of America, Great Britain, France and Japan, is contemplating, under certain conditions, a loan of $50,000,000.[4]

[1] The exact sum was 198,430,000 yen, according to *Millard's Review*, on Aug. 10, 1918. More loans have been made since then.

([2] Putnam-Weale, *The Fight for the Republic in China*, p. 379).

[3] Despite the most adverse conditions, the year 1917 was a very prosperous one, the maritime customs collections amounting to over $40,000,000, an increase of nearly $10,000,000 over those of the preceding year. The foreign trade in 1917 totalled more than a billion taels, which at the present rate of exchange equalled gold $1,032,699,412.

[4] The gravity of this economic situation from an international standpoint was clearly indicated in a recent article by Dr. Walter E. Weyl (*Harper's Magazine*, October, 1918):

"The urgent and increasing need of industrial progress renders all obstruction unavailing. The world is pressing in on

In the third place, the educational problem is a serious one. A comparatively small percentage of the Chinese can read or write their own language. The old system of education was classical and literary, and was open in fact only to a limited number; the new system will be practical and democratic, available for the many. In 1906, the first step was taken in this direction; but the new educational movement is too young to have attained its fullest success. Missionary insti-

China and the Chinese can no more hold off this advance then they can withstand modern artillery fire with their ancient city walls. Year by year the European nations acquire greater rights and wider powers; year by year they start new enterprises and secure new concessions, until the question comes to be not whether China will be developed, but merely whether the Chinese themselves will do the job or step aside and permit strangers to do it. Upon the answer to this question, upon China's proved capacity to take care of her own resources and utilize them wisely, hangs the immediate independence of China and her whole place in the world. China will either grow into an effective and capable industrial nation or will be held subject, at least temporarily, to international control and international exploitation. She will develop herself or be developed compulsorily by other nations in the interest of other nations. . . . Imperialism, which has divided up Africa and much of western Asia, now knocks at China's door. . . . How it will all end, by what means, if any, China will be enabled to hold her own, to develop herself and take her equal place among the great nations — is a baffling, haunting question, a challenge not only to the Chinese, but to those friends of China in the Western World who wish this problem to be settled justly and in peace."

tutions, staffed and financed largely by foreigners, have had a large share in the awakening of the people to the new learning, and still contribute much to the solving of the problem. The Central Ministry of Education has advised the teaching in all the schools of one form of the Chinese language — mandarin,— instead of the various dialects now prevalent. As in Japan, English is the best known foreign tongue, and is becoming the general language of the educated class, as French was once in universal use in Europe. A republic cannot exist without sufficient means of transportation, general education, and a strong sentiment of national patriotism, and all these requisites are to be gained only by a solution of the educational, economic and political problems of the nation.

The Chinese are among the first to admit that it will take a full generation to solve these problems, and to bring their nation within measurable distance of the present stage of civilization in other countries; but they believe they can solve them, if given time, and if freed from the menace of foreign attack or invasion of their rights, whether military, political or economic. They hope that the Peace Conference will guarantee them safety and freedom to work out their destiny unafraid. In brief, the Chinese feel that if the Allies will apply to the Orient the principles for which they are fighting in the present war, the future of their Republic will be secured.

Opposed to the out-and-out application of such principles to China, there have been suggested two alternatives, both of which are based on the assumption that the sovereign rights of the Chinese should be taken from them and given over to the foreign control, either of one, or of a group, of nations, which would undertake the development and control of China's resources and powers. A temporary supervision of her finances might be justified, but in general these alternatives do not seem to be in line with the international tendencies of the day; they would open the way for an imperialism which in turn might lead to new discords and international rivalries, as already indicated in an earlier portion of this chapter. The challenge is a direct one to the Chinese to prove by their unity and efficiency that this course should not be taken.

Instead of a further subtraction of the sovereign rights of the Chinese, the better course would seem to be in their gradual restoration — with possibly temporary assistance and regulation in an economic way,— somewhat along the lines indicated by Dr. Wellington Koo, the Chinese Minister, in his speech before the National Conference on Foreign Relations of the

United States held at Long Beach, N. Y., May 31st, 1917:

"What then is China's relation to the world's future? The answer really depends upon what policy the other nations adopt toward China, and what treatment they accord her. To be more definite, it depends upon whether they continue to permit themselves or any one of them, to commit one assault after another on her sovereignty; or seeing the injustice of these acts, acknowledge her right of existence and extend sympathy and support to her plans for progress. It depends upon whether they continue to keep the shackles of extra-territoriality, treaty tariffs, leased ports, railway zones and the like around her body; or, recognizing the unwisdom of such a policy, aid her to remove them and restore to her full liberty of development. It depends upon whether they remain indifferent to attempts on the part of some of them to revive the doctrine of the spheres of influence and to close the open door within her borders; or appreciating the ultimate consequences of such a course and the desirability of keeping the Chinese market open to international trade on a footing of equality, help China batter down this pernicious doctrine of spheres of influence, foil these selfish attempts, and maintain the principle of equal opportunity for the trade of all nations in all parts of China. It depends upon whether they permit any nation to wrest away her rich resources and immense man-power from her own possession, and utilize the one as means of aggrandizement and mould the other into instruments of conquest; or realizing the possibilities of danger to the peace of the Orient and the world, aid China to conserve these resources of wealth and power in her own hands and develop them, not as selfish means for aggression, but as instruments for the common purposes of peace. In short, it all depends upon whether they continue, in regard to China, to pursue a selfish policy of obstruction, interference and aggression, hoping thereby to get a share in whatever spoils may come; or whether they realize that such a course is sure to lead to conflicts, rivalry and antagonism, a disturbance of the peace of the nations; and that the best guarantee for the open-door policy, for the principle of equal opportunity and impartial trade for all, and for the devotion of her wonderful resources of wealth and power to peaceful purposes, lies in a strong and powerful China; and upon whether, realizing all this, they accord her that respect for her rights which they demand of her for their own rights, and conscientiously assist her to attain the end which is to be desired as much in the common interest of the world as for the sake of her own welfare."[1]

An out-and-out application of the principles of the Allies, as expressed especially by recent pronouncements of their statesmen, would seem to be the only course consistent with this point of view. The latest statements of the aims of the Allies were made by President Wilson on July 4, and on September 27th, 1918. On July 4th, he named four principles. The first was:

" The destruction of every arbitrary power anywhere that can separately, secretly, and of its single choice disturb the peace of the world; or, if it cannot at present be destroyed, at the least its reduction to virtual impotence."

Ever since the establishment of the Republic, China has been afraid of an attack by a foreign power; she has endeavoured to build up her military power; over half of her present income goes to the support of her military forces. If China could be assured, by a joint agreement of the nations, that the peace of the Far East could not be " separately and secretly disturbed " by any power, it could turn with a free mind to a solution of all of its internal problems of adjustment to the

[1] The New China and Her Relation to the World. *Proceedings of the Academy of Political Science,* Volume 7, No. 3.

present century. The money which is now being spent
to maintain its army could be invested in much needed
industrial development and improvement, and the progress of the whole country would be greatly accelerated.

The second principle enunciated by President Wilson
was:

" The settlement of every question, whether of territory, of sovereignty, of economic arrangement, or of
political relationship, upon the basis of the free acceptance of that settlement by the people immediately concerned, and not upon the basis of the material interests
or advantage of any other nation or people which may
desire a different settlement for the sake of its own
exterior influence or mastery."

This principle would have a most vital effect upon
China's future. Nearly every settlement, of territory,
of sovereignty, or of economic arrangement, with a
foreign power, in the past, with the exception of those
concluded with the United States, has been made upon
the basis of the " material interest or advantage " of
that power, and not " upon the basis of the free acceptance of that settlement " by China. Practically every
settlement has been made on an exactly opposite principle to that expressed by President Wilson. As a result, the present treaty-relations between China and
the other powers are distinctly disadvantageous to the

former. A typical Chinese view of the resulting inconsistencies appeared in *Millard's Review* of August 24th, 1918, written by Chuan Chao:

" Among the nations China has been least understood and most criticized. She tried to adapt herself to the western civilization by adopting the republican form of government. But the world Powers say that she is unfit because in the period of her reconstruction, as in that of France and of the United States after their revolutions, there is disorder. She attempted to live up to the open-door policy of John Hay. But the United States recognizes the special interests of Japan in China, especially in the places where her possessions are contiguous. After the foreign Powers have prevented her from developing her resources except according to their dictation, they blame her for industrial backwardness. After they have almost deprived her of tariff revenue, denied her the right of tariff legislation, forced her to lay heavy internal taxes on necessities, and burdened her with war loans for wars forced upon her, they blame her for financial insolvency. After they have negatived her territorial jurisdiction in the extraterritorial areas by lending these for the refuge of revolutionists, hot-beds of intrigue and sources of vice, they blame her for governmental inefficiency. After they have forced her to raze all fortifications between the capital and the sea, leased the important ports for their naval stations and stationed troops constantly on Chinese soil, they blame her for military impotency. As a friendly neighbour, she was presented a series of twenty-one demands. As a neutral, her territory was invaded in spite of her protest. As an ally of the Entente, her alliance has been utilized for the consolidation of one of her ally's position in China."

This viewpoint is perhaps open to criticism, as many of the treaty agreements mentioned were the result of infringements by China of the rights of other nations. But there seems to be little question of the necessity of revising the treaties if justice is to be done. This course has been strongly advocated by both Chinese and American and British economists and writers. Thus Dr. M. T. Z. Tyau, writing in 1917, names two reasons for this revision; first because of the vagueness of the wording of the present treaties which have caused and will cause serious misunderstanding; and secondly, because most of the obligations were contracted half a century ago, so that they now " fetter the free growth and the natural development of the new Republic, to the serious menace of even its self-preservation. . . . If peace in the Far East, as well as the rest of the world, is to be preserved, the contracting parties will have to treat one another with equal respect and consideration. The injustices, the inequalities, the inconsistencies of the past, must be abolished, and rational bases of mutual intercourse substituted"[1] Dr. Wu Ting-fang, writing in a similar vein, said: "We have heard the public pronouncements of the statesmen of the powers, that after the war, justice and equality will rule among the nations. We believe in them, and have great hopes of them. We expect that in carrying them out into practice in China, one of the first things that will be done will be a reasonable and equitable revision of our treaties."[2] Doctor S. K. Hornbeck, speaking before the National Conference on Foreign Relations of the United States, June 1st, 1917, said: "Various of the old far-eastern agreements should, by international agreement, be legislated out of existence. There should be a cleaning of the old slate, with its entries of individualism. There should be new agreements, entered into by all the interested powers, drafted on the principle of fair play for all, with full respect for the rights of all, and establishing effective limitations upon the hitherto assumed right of each state, because independent, to act inde-

[1] *Legal Obligations Arising out of Treaty Relations between China and other States*, pages 207–217.
[2] Introduction to above, page 8.

pendently and with a view to its own peculiar and selfish interests." Mr. B. L. Putnam-Weale, a British writer, has asserted that " the entire politico-economic relationship between the Republic and the world, must be remodelled at the earliest possible opportunity; every agreement which has been made since the Treaties of 1860 being carefully and completely revised." [1]

Finally, the friendship between China and Japan would be increased if their economic relations were governed by the principle of voluntary mutual agreement. There has been growing up a cloud of suspicion and distrust between the two countries which only a recognition of such a principle can clear away. If this principle were recognized and upheld, an important step forward would be taken toward making the peace of the Orient secure.

President Wilson's third principle was:

" The consent of all nations to be governed in a conduct toward each other by the same principles of honour and of respect for the common law of civilized society that govern the individual citizens of all modern States in their relations with one another; to the end that all promises and covenants may be sacredly observed, no private plots or conspiracies hatched, no

---

[1] Putnam-Weale, *The Fight for the Republic in China*, page 375.

Dr. V. K. Wellington Koo, Chinese Minister to America, after receiving an Honorary Degree from Columbia University in 1917.

Dr. Koo is a graduate of Columbia University and has received the degree of Doctor of Philosophy from that institution He is the youngest member of the Diplomatic Corps at Washington. On his left is Professor John Bassett Moore of Columbia University.

selfish injuries wrought with impunity, and a mutual trust established upon the handsome foundation of a mutual respect for right."

The present situation in China is analogous in a lesser degree to that in Russia; both countries offer supreme opportunities for exploitation, or for disinterested assistance. Like Russia, China needs help. She needs help in every phase of her new life. She looks to the Occident for that help; and if this principle were applied, she would not look in vain. The definite assistance which other countries, and especially America, could give China, was outlined by C. T. Wang, formerly Vice President of the Senate, in a speech made in 1917. This speech was delivered before the Lansing-Ishii Agreement was concluded. Mr. Wang suggested political, financial and industrial assistance. His remarks were made just after the attempted restoration of the Manchus, when there seemed to be doubt as to the ability of the Republic to survive, without external assistance. Mr. Wang said:

"In this vital struggle, where shall America, the champion of democracy, stand? We entirely agree with Mr. Millard (an eminent journalist) in his views expressed through the editorial columns in the last issue of his paper, which we will reproduce here for emphasis:

" ' A primary requisite is that, as between reversion to an archaic monarchy, or the retention of a military oligarchy, or a graduated advance toward genuine republicanism, the influence of the United States ought to be thrown definitely to bring about the latter alternative. If this leads to quasi-interference in Chinese politics, then that responsibility must be faced. It is becoming rather ridiculous, at a time when America is engaged in a world-war, when the whole life of the American people is being readjusted to meet these war conditions, and with the avowed principal object of saving democratic principle of government from being smothered by autocratic militarism, that the power and influence of the United States should be applied in one place abroad, and should not be applied in another place abroad; that direct American assistance should be accorded to some nations that are trying to cast off the yoke of autocracy, and be denied to other nations that are making the same effort.'

" Besides political assistance America is also in an excellent position to aid China financially — of which she stands so much in need.

" A third way in which America can help China is to bring into China a sufficient number of experts who can aid China to establish and develop large industrial plants and factories and to train and bring up a large

THE FUTURE OF CHINA

force of native industrial and technical leaders. " We beg to advance these three ways for America to aid China. The political assistance aims to renew the open door policy and to influence the Entente Powers to maintain the same principles of liberty, constitutionalism and democracy in China as they are fighting to maintain on the battlefield of Europe. The financial aid is to be directed at the industrial, commercial and other productive development of the country. The introduction of industrial and technical experts has for its objective the improved methods of administration of existing revenue-producing organs of the government, the establishment of other productive organizations, and the training of Chinese youths in sufficient numbers to direct, maintain and develop such organizations." [1]

[1] Note on Investment of Foreign Capital in China.
The following extract is taken from an address by Dr. S. K. Hornbeck before the National Conference on Foreign Relations of the United States at Long Beach, N. Y., June 1st, 1917.
"China needs capital. She must get it, she is eager to have it. She has repeatedly asked it of us. Without capital she cannot develop her resources. Upon the development of her resources depends the increasing of her power to sell and to buy. Upon this depends her economic and probably her political salvation. All this means that there must be investments — capital from abroad. But investments in China require, under existing conditions, the giving and taking of concessions, with a certain amount of foreign supervision. There is noth-

The final principle before the Allies was:
" The establishment of an organization of peace
which shall make it certain that the combined power of
free nations will check every invasion of right, and
serve to make peace and justice the more secure, by

ing inherently evil in the process. The thing that is desirable
is that investments and concessions — those on a large scale at
least — be subjected to regulation. The present evil lies in absence of regulations, in extreme individualism. There should
be regulation through a group of governments — including the
Chinese — on a basis of co-operation. We should offer our
capital only where we are assured that it will not be used to
further political ends of which we do not approve. If we think
to avert rather than to precipitate conflict, if we are seriously
interested in the problem of developing China's resources with
a minimum of friction, we must work for something more
promising than a new application of the old individualistic principle. . . . This suggests nothing short of general, that is, extended, international co-operation for the placing of capital in
China. . . . It would require frank co-operation on the part of
the governments of those states which have capital for foreign
investment. . . . As a group, the co-operating states, including
and with the consent of China, could determine the distribution
and guarantee the security of capital accepted for Chinese enterprises. . . . Administration of special securities, where required, should be subject to international personnel, after the
model of the Chinese Customs Service. It should be understood that no concession should be taken and no investment
be made which had not the approval of the Chinese government.
. . . If there is any region in the world today in which it is
practicable to attempt the experiment of a league of forces,
economic and political, for the preservation of the peace, that
region is to be found in the field which has long been a battle

affording a definite tribunal of opinion to which all must submit, and by which every international readjustment that cannot be amicably agreed upon by the peoples directly concerned, shall be sanctioned."

Both China and Japan desire inclusion in the membership of this "league of nations." If they are not thus included, a new international alignment may occur, which would have potential possibilities for a new outbreak of hostilities. The question has been put directly to Japan as to the possibilities of an alliance with Germany, after the war, and Premier Terauchi answered that this were possible only if Japan found herself isolated from the rest of the powers. In a written interview published in the *Outlook* (New York) of May 1st, 1918, in reply to the question of Mr. Mason, a representative of the *Outlook*, " What are the chances for an alliance between Japan and Germany?" Count Terauchi replied: " That will depend entirely on how the present war may end. It is impossible to predict the changes which the conclusion of the

ground of trade, concessions and investments — the Far East."
F. N. (*Proceedings of the Academy of Political Science* (N. Y.), Vol. VII, No. 3, pp. 92–98).

The announcement made on July 29th of the intention of the United States Government to support bankers in joining in a loan of $50,000,000, with Great Britain, France and Japan, seems to be in line with these principles.

war may bring.   If the exigencies of international relationships demand it, Japan, *being unable to maintain
a position of total isolation,* may be induced to seek an
ally in Germany.   But, as far as I can judge from the
existing conditions of affairs, I see no such danger.
In other words, I believe that Japan's relations with the
Entente Allies will continue unaltered after the present
war."

This statement of the Premier has been generally
criticized by the Japanese press, and on Sept. 30th he
was succeeded by Kei Hara, a commoner, and the
leader of the Seiyukai Party (constitutionalists), but
it indicates a possibility which might develop in the
Orient if the nations there are not included in a world-
organization.   If such a world-league and a tribunal
of world opinion were set up, it would at once prevent
any new acts of aggression against either Japan or
China.   Such a solution would be a welcome one.
China especially is pacific, and its ideals are in line with
those of such an organization.   Dr. W. C. Dennis, the
new American Legal Adviser to the Chinese Government, in August, voiced the approval of the Chinese of
such a proposed league.   After discussing its possibilities and its drawbacks, he said:

" The proposed plan, if practicable, is of the greatest possible interest to those nations which, like the

United States and China, have, taking their history as a whole, consciously sought the victories of peace rather than those of war. It is in accordance with the genius of their institutions and the desires of their peoples." [1]

On September 27th, 1918, President Wilson again expressed the attitude of the American Government toward Peace. His main emphasis was upon the necessity of absolute justice regardless of whom this principle might affect; upon the necessity of absolute publicity of all treaties and agreements; and a decided opposition to any special alliances or economic combinations within the league itself. All these conditions have a peculiar applicability to the situation in the Orient, especially in reference to China. At times there seems to be a tendency on the part of the American and European public to be indifferent to the fate of the Orientals, but President Wilson's first condition was that " impartial justice which is meted out must involve no discrimination between those to whom we wish to be just and those to whom we do not wish to be just. It must be a justice that plays no favourites and knows no standard but the equal rights of the several peoples concerned." Further, there has seemed

[1] From the *Chinese Social and Political Science Review,* quoted in *Millard's Review,* Aug. 10, 1918.

to be a disposition on the part of people in the Occidental world to allow Japan, or any other nation or group of nations, to make any terms which they could with China, but President Wilson's second principle would rule this out, as "no special or separate interest of any single nation or any group of nations can be made the basis of any part of the settlement which is not consistent with the common interests of all." The principle of the "open door" and "equal opportunity" would be enforced by the third and fourth requirements of this Allied peace program; namely, that "there can be no leagues or alliance or special covenants and understandings within the general and common family by the league of nations; or specifically there can be no special, selfish economic combinations within the league and no employment of any form of economic boycott or exclusion except as the power of economic penalty by exclusion from the markets of the world may be vested in the league of nations itself as a means of discipline and control." Finally, there are to be no more secret agreements, as "all international agreements and treaties of every kind must be made known in their entirety to the rest of the world." This point alone would free the relations of China and Japan from much of the suspicion which is gathered about the secret negotiations following the Twenty-one Demands, the Sino-Japanese Military Agreement, and frequent accusations of the Chinese press that their officials were about to " sell China " to Japan.

Summarizing his principles in the form of questions, President Wilson, on Sept. 27th, said, " Shall strong nations be free to wrong weak nations and make them subject to their purpose and interest? Shall there be a common standard of right and privilege for all peoples and nations, or shall the wrong do as they will and the weak suffer without regrets? " As if in answer to these questions comes the cry of Kang Yu-wei and his countrymen from the other side of the world: " There is no such thing as an army of righteousness which will come to the assistance of weak nations! " [1] The issue for the Orient as well as the Occident seems to be clear-cut. The President has said: " These issues must be settled — by no arrangement or compromise or adjustment of interests, but definitely and once for all and with a full and unequivocal acceptance of the principle that the interest of the weakest is as sacred as the interest of the strongest."

No human being can view the incalculable loss of human life and wealth that is being wrought by the Great War, and remain unmoved. " For what purpose is this waste? " Only in the achievement of some

[1] See page 85.

such principles as given above can any such loss be reconciled. These principles must be no less than worldwide in their application; they should extend not only to the free peoples of Europe and America, but also to the newborn democracies of the Mongol and the Slav. Especially do they concern the vast republic across the Pacific, whose future relations with the rest of the world are so full of potential possibilities for discord or for peace. The importance of these relations was summarized twenty years ago by John Hay in two sentences: " The storm-centre of the world has gradually shifted to China. . . . Whoever understands that mighty Empire socially, politically, economically, religiously, has a key to world-politics for the next five centuries." Against the background of the great democratic upheavals in the East that are just beginning to take concrete shape and expression, and of the costly cataclysm in the West which seems at last to be nearing its concluding phases, these statements have a new meaning, both as a warning and a prophecy, concerning the new age which is to come.

APPENDICES

APPENDICES

1. The "Black-Dragon" Statement of Japanese Policy in China as a result of the European War. (Written in 1914.)

2. Documents relating to the Twenty-one Demands made by Japan on China, in 1915.

3. Official Statements in Relation to the Lansing-Ishii Agreement between America and Japan concerning China, in 1917.

4. Summary of Treaties and Agreements with Reference to the Integrity and Sovereign Rights of China, and the "Open Door" Policy and "Equality of Opportunities."

5. Summary of Treaties and Agreements with Reference to Korea.

An Introductory Bibliography on China.

APPENDIX I

THE "BLACK-DRAGON" STATEMENT OF JAPANESE POLICY IN CHINA AS A RESULT OF THE EUROPEAN WAR. (WRITTEN IN 1914.)

EXPLANATORY NOTE

THE following statement of Japanese foreign policy was surprisingly accurate in its forecasting of future events. It is interesting to note how these events are suggested in this paper. The statement is made that on account of the absorption of the European nations in the Great War, "now is the most opportune moment for Japan to quickly solve the Chinese question. We should by all means decide and act at once." Within a month, or two months after this statement was made, the Twenty-one Demands were served on China. Most of their terms were mentioned in the list of objections under the "Secret Terms of the Defensive Alliance." This Defensive Alliance was eventually concluded three years later in May, 1918. The share of Japan in assisting the revolutionists to stir up trouble in China was also mentioned. "We should induce the Chinese Revolutionists, the Imperialists and other Chinese malcontents to create trouble all over China." Yuan Shih-kai was considered an avowed enemy of Japan; and the Black Dragon Society advised his overthrow. "The whole country will be thrown into disorder and Yuan's Government will consequently be overthrown." The Agreement concluded with Russia in 1916 was forecasted in the statement: "At this moment it is of paramount importance for Japan to come to a special understanding with Russia to define our respective spheres in Manchuria and Mongolia so that the two countries may co-operate with each other in the future." The Lansing-Ishii agreement in 1917 was suggested in the phrases: "what Japan must now somewhat reckon with is America; but America in her attitude towards us regarding our policy toward China has already declared the principle of maintaining China's territorial integrity and equal opportunity, and will be satisfied, if we do not impair America's already acquired rights and privileges." Even the very phrases which Count Terauchi used in May, 1918, in answer to the question as to the possibility of a Japanese alliance with Germany appeared in this document. "Japan will be isolated from the European powers after the war, and will be regarded by them with envy and jealousy just as Germany is now regarded."

Thus practically all the great decisions in Japanese foreign policy since the Great War, as they affected her relations with China, with Russia, and with America, were forecasted in this Black Dragon Memorandum. Consequently, the statement as a whole, and any objectives it mentions, which have not as yet been reached, have more than an ordinary interest.

THE BLACK DRAGON MEMORANDUM

PART I. THE EUROPEAN WAR AND THE CHINESE QUESTION

The present gigantic struggle in Europe has no parallel in history. Not only will the equilibrium of Europe be affected and its effect felt all over the globe, but its results will create a New Era in the political and social world. Therefore, whether or not the Imperial Japanese Government can settle the Far Eastern Question and bring to realization our great Imperial policy depends on our being able to skilfully avail ourselves of the world's general trend of affairs so as to extend our influence and to decide upon a course of action towards China which shall be practical in execution. If our authorities and people view the present European War with indifference and without deep concern, merely devoting their attention to the attack on Kiaochow, neglecting the larger issues of the war, they will have brought to naught our great Imperial policy, and committed a blunder greater than which it can not be conceived. We are constrained to submit this statement of policy for the consideration of our authorities, not because we are fond of argument but because we are deeply anxious for our national welfare.

No one at present can foretell the outcome of the European War. If the Allies meet with reverses and victory shall crown the arms of the Germans and Austrians, German militarism will undoubtedly dominate the European Continent and extend southward and eastward to other parts of the world. Should such a state of affairs happen to take place the consequences resulting therefrom will be indeed great and extensive. On this account we must devote our most serious attention to the subject. If, on the other hand, the Germans and Austrians should be crushed by the Allies, Germany will be deprived of her present status as a Federated State under a Kaiser. The Federation will be disintegrated into separate states and Prussia will have to be content with the status of a second-rate Power. Austria and Hungary, on account of this defeat, will consequently be divided. What their final fate will be, no one would now venture to predict. In the meantime Russia will annex Galicia and the Austrian Poland; France will repossess Alsace and Lorraine; Great Britain will occupy the German Colonies in Africa and the South Pacific: Servia and Montenegro will take Bosnia, Herzegovina and a certain portion of Austrian territory; thus making such great changes in the map of Europe that even the Napoleonic War in 1815 could not find a parallel.

When these events take place, not only will Europe experience great changes, but we should not ignore the fact that they will occur also in China and in the South Pacific. After Russia has replaced Germany in the territories lost by Germany and Austria, she will hold a controlling influence in Europe, and, for a long time to come, will have nothing to fear from her western frontier. Immediately after the war she will make an effort to carry out her policy of expansion in the East and will not relax her effort until she has acquired a controlling influence in China. At the same time, Great Britain will strengthen her position in the Yangtze Valley and prohibit any other country from getting a footing there. France will do likewise in Yunnan province, using it as her base of operations for further encroachments upon China and never hesitate to extend her advantages. We must therefore seriously study the situation, remembering always that the combined action of Great Britain, Russia and France will not only affect Europe but that we can even foresee that it will also affect China.

Whether this combined action on the part of England, France and Russia is to terminate at the end of the war or to continue to operate, we can not now predict. But after peace in Europe is restored, these Powers will certainly turn their attention to the expansion of their several spheres of interest in China, and, in the adjustment, their interests will most likely conflict with one another. If their interests do not conflict, they will work jointly to solve the Chinese Question. On this point we have not the least doubt. If England, France and Russia are actually to combine for the coercion of China, what course is to be adopted by the Imperial Japanese Government to meet the situation? What proper means shall we employ to maintain our influence and extend our interests within this ring of rivalry and competition? It is necessary that we bear in mind the final results of the European War and forestall the trend of events succeeding it so as to be able to decide upon a policy towards China and determine the action to be ultimately taken. If we remain passive, the Imperial Japanese Government's policy towards China will lose that subjective influence and our diplomacy will be checked forever by the combined force of the other Powers. The peace of the Far East will be thus endangered and even the existence of the Japanese Empire as a nation will no doubt be imperiled. It is therefore our first important duty at this moment to enquire of our Government what course is to be adopted to face that general situation after the war. What preparations are being made to meet the combined pressure of the Allies upon China? What policy has been followed to solve the Chinese Question? When the European War is terminated and peace restored we are not concerned so much with the question whether it be the Dual Monarchies or the Triple Entente which emerge victorious, but whether, in anticipation of the future expansion of European influence in the Continents of Europe and Asia, the Imperial Japanese Government should or should not hesitate to employ force to check the movement before this occurrence. Now is the most opportune moment for Japan to quickly solve the Chinese Question. Such an opportunity will not occur for hundreds of years to come. Not only is it Japan's divine duty to act now, but present conditions in China favour the execution of such a plan. We should by all means decide and act at once. If our authorities do not avail themselves of this rare opportunity, great duty will surely be encountered in future in the settlement of this Chinese question. *Japan will be isolated* from the European Powers after the war, and will be regarded by them with envy and jealousy just as Germany is now regarded. Is it not then a vital necessity for Japan to solve at this very moment the Chinese Question?

PART II. THE CHINESE QUESTION AND THE DEFENSIVE ALLIANCE

It is a very important matter of policy whether the Japanese Government, in obedience to its divine mission, shall solve the Chinese Question in a heroic manner by making China voluntarily rely upon Japan. To force China to such a position there is nothing else for the Imperial Japanese Government to do but to take advantage of the present opportunity to seize the reins of political and financial power and to enter by all means into a defensive alliance with her under secret terms as enumerated below:

The Secret Terms of the Defensive Alliance

The Imperial Japanese Government, with due respect for the Sovereignty and Integrity of China and with the object and hope of maintaining the peace of the Far East, undertakes to share the responsibility of co-operating with China to guard her against internal trouble and foreign invasion and China shall accord to

Japan special facilities in the matter of China's National Defence, or the protection of Japan's special rights and privileges and for these objects the following treaty of Alliance is to be entered into between the two contracting parties:

1. When there is internal trouble in China or when she is at war with another nation or nations, Japan shall send her army to render assistance, to assume the responsibility of guarding Chinese territory and to maintain peace and order in China.

2. China agrees to recognize Japan's privileged position in South Manchuria and Inner Mongolia and to cede the sovereign rights of these regions to Japan to enable her to carry out a scheme of local defence on a permanent basis.

3. After the Japanese occupation of Kiaochow, Japan shall acquire all the rights and privileges heretofore enjoyed by the Germans in regard to railways, mines and all other interests, and after peace and order is restored in Tsingtao, the place shall be handed back to China to be opened as an International Treaty port.

4. For the maritime defence of China and Japan, China shall lease strategic harbours along the coast of the Fukien province to Japan to be converted into naval bases and grant to Japan in the said province all railway and mining rights.

5. For the reorganization of the Chinese army China shall entrust the training and drilling of the army to Japan.

6. For the unification of China's firearms and munitions of war, China shall adopt firearms of Japanese pattern, and at the same time establish arsenals (with the help of Japan) in different strategic points.

7. With the object of creating and maintaining a Chinese Navy, China shall entrust the training of her navy to Japan.

8. With the object of reorganizing her finances and improving the methods of taxation, China shall entrust the work to Japan, and the latter shall elect competent financial experts who shall act as first-class advisers to the Chinese Government.

9. China shall engage Japanese educational experts as educational advisers and extensively establish schools in different parts of the country to teach Japanese so as to raise the educational standard of the country.

10. China shall first consult with and obtain the consent of Japan before she can enter into an agreement with another Power for making loans, the leasing of territory, or the cession of the same.

From the date of the signing of this Defensive Alliance, Japan and China shall work together hand-in-hand. Japan will assume the responsibility of safeguarding Chinese territory and maintaining the peace and order in China. This will relieve China of all future anxieties and enable her to proceed energetically with her reforms, and, with a sense of territorial security, she may wait for her national development and regeneration. Even after the present European War is over and peace is restored China will absolutely have nothing to fear in the future of having pressure brought against her by the foreign powers. It is only thus that permanent peace can be secured in the Far East.

But before concluding this Defensive Alliance, two points must first be ascertained and settled. (1) Its bearing on the Chinese Government. (2) Its bearing on those Powers having intimate relations with, and great interests in, China.

In considering its effect on the Chinese Government, Japan must try to foresee whether the position of China's present ruler Yuan Shih-kai shall be permanent or not; whether the present Government's policy will enjoy the confidence of a large section of the Chinese people; whether Yuan Shih-kai will readily agree to the Japanese Government's proposal to enter into a treaty of alliance with us. These are points to which we are bound to give a thorough consideration. Judging by the attitude hitherto adopted by Yuan Shih-kai we know he has always resorted to the policy of expediency in his diplomatic dealings, and although he may outwardly show friendliness towards us, he will in fact rely upon the influence of the different Powers as the easiest check against us and refuse to accede to our demands. Take for a single instance, his conduct towards us since the Imperial Government declared war against Germany and his action will then be clear to all. Whether we can rely upon the ordinary friendly methods of diplomacy to gain our object or not it does not require much wisdom to decide. After the gigantic struggle in Europe is over, leaving aside America, which will not press for advantage, China will not be able to obtain any loans from the other Powers. With a depleted treasury, without means to pay the officials and the army, with local bandits inciting the poverty-stricken populace to trouble, with the revolutionists waiting for opportunities to rise, should an insurrection actually occur while no outside assistance can be rendered to quell it we are certain it will be impossible for Yuan Shih-kai, single-handed, to restore order and consolidate the country. The result will be that the nation will be cut up into many parts beyond all hope of remedy. That this state of affairs will come is not difficult to foresee. When this occurs, shall we uphold Yuan's Government and assist him to suppress the internal insurrection with the certain assurance that we could influence him to agree to our demands, or shall we help the revolutionists to achieve a success and realize our object through them? This question must be definitely decided upon this very moment so that we may put it into practical execution. If we do not look into the future fate of China but go blindly to uphold Yuan's Government, to enter into a Defensive Alliance with China, hoping thus to secure a complete realization of our object by assisting him to suppress the revolutionists, it is obviously a wrong policy. Why? Because the majority of the Chinese people have lost all faith in the tottering Yuan Shih-

kai who is discredited and attacked by the whole nation for having sold his country. If Japan gives Yuan
the support, his Government, though in a very precarious state, may possibly avoid destruction. Yuan
Shih-kai belongs to that school of politicians who are
fond of employing craftiness and cunning. He may
be friendly to us for a time, but he will certainly abandon us and again befriend the other Powers when the
European war is at an end. Judging by his past we
have no doubt as to what he will do in the future. For
Japan to ignore the general sentiment of the Chinese
people and support Yuan Shih-kai with the hope that
we can settle with him the Chinese Question is a blunder indeed. Therefore, in order to secure the permanent peace of the Far East, instead of supporting a
Chinese Government which can neither be long continued in power nor assist in the attainment of our object, we should rather support the 400,000,000 Chinese people to renovate their corrupt Government, to
change its present form, to maintain peace and order
in the land and to usher into China a new era of prosperity so that China and Japan may in fact as well as
in name be brought into the most intimate and vital
relations with each other. China's era of prosperity
is based on the Chino-Japanese Alliance and this Alliance is the foundational power for the repelling of
the foreign aggression that is to be directed against
the Far East at the conclusion of the European War.
This Alliance is also the foundation-stone of the peace
of the world. Japan therefore should take this as the

last warning and immediately solve this question. Since the Imperial Japanese Government has considered it imperative to support the Chinese people, we should induce the Chinese revolutionists, the Imperialists and other Chinese malcontents to create trouble all over China. The whole country will be thrown into disorder and Yuan's Government will consequently be overthrown. We shall then select a man from amongst the most influential and most noted of the 400,000,000 of Chinese and help him to organize a new form of Government and to consolidate the whole country. In the meantime our army must assist in the restoration of peace and order in the country, and in the protection of the lives and properties of the people, so that they may gladly tender their allegiance to the new Government which will then naturally confide in and rely upon Japan. It is after the accomplishment of only these things that we shall without difficulty gain our object by the conclusion of a Defensive Alliance with China.

For us to incite the Chinese revolutionists and malcontents to rise in China we consider the present to be the most opportune moment. The reason why these men can not now carry on an active campaign is because they are insufficiently provided with funds. If the Imperial Government can take advantage of this fact to make them a loan and instruct them to rise simultaneously, great commotion and disorder will surely prevail all over China. We can intervene and easily adjust matters.

The progress of the European War warns Japan with greater urgency of the imperative necessity of solving this most vital of questions. The Imperial Government can not be considered as embarking on a rash project. This opportunity will not repeat itself for our benefit. We must avail ourselves of this chance and under no circumstances hesitate. Why should we wait for the spontaneous uprising of the revolutionists and malcontents? Why should we not think out and lay down a plan beforehand? When we examine into the form of government in China, we must ask whether the existing Republic is well suited to the national temperament and well adapted to the thoughts and aspirations of the Chinese people. From the time the Republic of China was established up to the present moment, if what it has passed through is to be compared to what it ought to be in the matter of administration and unification, we find disappointment everywhere. Even the revolutionists themselves, the very ones who first advocated the Republican form of government, acknowledge that they have made a mistake. The retention of the Republican form of Government in China will be a great future obstacle in the way of a Chino-Japanese alliance. And why must it be so? Because, in a Republic the fundamental principles of government as well as the social and moral aims of the people are distinctly different from that of a Constitutional Monarchy. Their laws and administration also conflict. If Japan act as a guide to China and China model herself after Japan, it will only then be possible for the two nations to solve by mutual effort the Far East Question without differences and disagreements. Therefore, to start from the foundation for the purpose of reconstructing the Chinese Government, of establishing a Chino-Japanese Alliance, of maintaining the permanent peace of the Far East and of realizing the consummation of Japan's Imperial policy, we must take advantage of the present opportunity to alter China's Republican form of Government into a Constitutional Monarchy which shall necessarily be identical, in all its details, to the Constitutional Monarchy of Japan, and to no other. This is really the key and first principle to be firmly held for the actual reconstruction of the form of Government in China. If China changes her Republican form of Government to that of a Constitutional Monarchy, shall we, in the selection of a new ruler, restore the Emperor Hsuan T'ung to his throne or choose the most capable man from the Monarchists or select the most worthy member from among the revolutionists? We think, however, that it is advisable at present to leave this question to the exigency of the future when the matter is brought up for decision. But we must not lose sight of the fact that to actually put into execution this policy of a Chino-Japanese Alliance and the transformation of the Republic of China into a Constitutional Monarchy, is, in reality, the fundamental principle to be adopted for the reconstruction of China.

We shall now consider the bearing of this Defensive

Alliance on the other Powers. Needless to say, Japan and China will in no way impair the rights and interests already acquired by the Powers. At this moment it is of paramount importance for Japan to come to a special understanding with Russia to define our respective spheres in Manchuria and Mongolia so that the two countries may co-operate with each other in the future. This means that Japan after the acquisition of sovereign rights in South Manchuria and Inner Mongolia will work together with Russia after her acquisition of sovereign rights in North Manchuria and Outer Mongolia to maintain the status quo, and endeavour by every effort to protect the peace of the Far East. Russia, since the outbreak of the European War, has not only laid aside all ill-feelings against Japan, but has adopted the same attitude as her Allies and shown warm friendship for us. No matter how we regard the Manchurian and Mongolian Questions in the future she is anxious that we find some way of settlement. Therefore we need not doubt but that Russia, in her attitude towards this Chinese Question, will be able to come to an understanding with us for mutual co-operation.

The British sphere of influence and interest in China is centred in Tibet and the Yangtsze Valley. Therefore, if Japan can come to some satisfactory arrangement with China in regard to Tibet and also give certain privileges to Great Britain in the Yangtze Valley, with an assurance to protect those privileges, no matter how powerful Great Britain might be, she will surely not oppose Japan's policy in regard to this Chinese Question. While this present European War is going on Great Britain has never asked Japan to render her assistance. That her strength will certainly not enable her to oppose us in the future need not be doubted in the least.

Since Great Britain and Russia will not oppose Japan's policy towards China, it can readily be seen what attitude France will adopt in regard to the subject. What Japan must now somewhat reckon with is America. But America in her attitude towards us regarding our policy towards China has already declared the principle of maintaining China's territorial integrity and equal opportunity and will be satisfied, if we do not impair America's already acquired rights and privileges. We think America will also have no cause for complaint. Nevertheless America has in the East a naval force which can be fairly relied upon, though not sufficiently strong to be feared. Therefore in Japan's attitude towards America there is nothing really for us to be afraid of.

Since China's condition is such on the one hand and the Powers' relation towards China is such on the other hand, Japan should avail herself in the meantime of the European War to definitely decide upon a policy towards China, the most important move being the transformation of the Chinese Government to be followed up by preparing for the conclusion of the Defensive Alliance. The precipitate action on the part of our present Cabinet in acceding to the request of Great Britain to declare war against Germany without having definitely settled our policy towards China has no real connection with our future negotiations with China or affects the political condition in the Far East. Consequently, all intelligent Japanese, of every walk of life throughout the land, are very deeply concerned about the matter.

Our Imperial Government should now definitely change our dependent foreign policy which is being directed by others into an independent foreign policy which shall direct others, proclaiming the same with solemn sincerity to the world and carrying it out with determination. If we do so, even the gods and spirits will give way. These are important points in our policy towards China and the result depends on how we carry them out. Can our authorities firmly make up their mind to solve this Chinese Question by the actual carrying out of this fundamental principle? If they show irresolution while we have this heaven-conferred chance and merely depend on the good will of the other Powers, we shall eventually have greater pressure to be brought against the Far East after the European War is over, when the present equilibrium will be destroyed. That day will then be too late for us to repent our folly. We are therefore impelled by force of circumstances to urge our authorities to a quicker sense of the situation and to come to a determination.

Translation from *The Fight for the Republic in China*, by B. L. Putnam-Weale. (Copyright 1917 by Dodd, Mead & Company, Inc.)

APPENDIX II

DOCUMENTS RELATING TO THE TWENTY-ONE DE-
MANDS MADE BY JAPAN ON CHINA IN 1915.

(A) JAPAN'S REVISED DEMANDS ON CHINA

Presented April 26, 1915
Following the original Twenty-one Demands on China
presented Jan. 18, 1915

NOTE ON ORIGINAL TEXT

(The revised list of articles is a Chinese translation
of the Japanese text. It is hereby declared that when
a final decision is reached, there shall be a revision of
the wording of the text.)

GROUP I

The Japanese Government and the Chinese Government, being desirous of maintaining the general peace
in Eastern Asia and further strengthening the friendly
relations and good neighbourhood existing between the
two nations, agree to the following articles:

Art. 1. The Chinese Government engages to give
full assent to all matters upon which the Japanese
Government may hereafter agree with the German
Government, relating to the disposition of all rights,

interests and concessions, which Germany, by virtue of treaties or otherwise, possesses in relation to the Province of Shantung.

Art. 2. (Changed into an exchange of notes.)

The Chinese Government declares that within the Province of Shantung and along its coast no territory or island will be ceded or leased to any Power under any pretext.

Art. 3. The Chinese Government consents that as regards the railway to be built by China herself from Chefoo or Lungkow to connect with the Kiaochow-Tsinanfu Railway, if Germany is willing to abandon the privilege of financing the Chefoo-Weihsien line, China will approach Japanese capitalists to negotiate for a loan.

Art. 4. The Chinese Government engages, in the interest of trade and for the residence of foreigners, to open by China herself as soon as possible certain suitable places in the Province of Shantung as Commercial Ports.

(Supplementary Exchange of Notes)

The places which ought to be opened are to be chosen and the regulations are to be drafted, by the Chinese Government, but the Japanese Minister must be consulted before making a decision.

GROUP II

The Japanese Government and the Chinese Government, with a view to developing their economic relations in South Manchuria and Eastern Inner Mongolia, agree to the following articles:

Art. 1. The two contracting Powers mutually agree that the term of lease of Port Arthur and Dalny and the terms of the South Manchuria Railway and the Antung-Mukden Railway shall be extended to 99 years.

(Supplementary Exchange of Notes)

The term of lease of Port Arthur and Dalny shall expire in the 86th year of the Republic or 1997. The date for restoring the South Manchurian Railway to China shall fall due in the 91st year of the Republic or 2002. Article 12 in the original South Manchurian Railway Agreement stating that it may be redeemed by China after 36 years after the traffic is opened is hereby cancelled. The term of the Antung-Mukden Railway shall expire in the 96th year of the Republic or 2007.

Art. 2. Japanese subjects in South Manchuria may lease or purchase the necessary land for erecting suitable buildings for trade and manufacture or for prosecuting agricultural enterprises.

Art. 3. Japanese subjects shall be free to reside and travel in South Manchuria and to engage in business and manufacture of any kind whatsoever.

Art. 3-a. The Japanese subjects referred to in the preceding two articles, besides being required to register with the local authorities pass-ports which they must procure under the existing regulations, shall also submit to police laws and ordinances and tax regulations, which are approved by the Japanese consul. Civil and criminal cases in which the defendants are Japanese shall be tried and adjudicated by the Japanese consul; those in which the defendants are Chinese shall be tried and adjudicated by Chinese Authorities. In either case an officer can be deputed to the court to attend the proceedings. But mixed civil cases between Chinese and Japanese relating to land shall be tried and adjudicated by delegates of both nations conjointly in accordance with Chinese law and local usage. When the judicial system in the said region is completely reformed, all civil and criminal cases concerning Japanese subjects shall be tried entirely by Chinese law courts.

Art. 4. (Changed to an exchange of notes.)

The Chinese Government agrees that Japanese subjects shall be permitted forthwith to investigate, select, and then prospect for and open mines at the following places in South Manchuria, apart from those mining areas in which mines are being prospected for or worked; until the Mining Ordinance is definitely settled methods at present in force shall be followed.

PROVINCE OF FENG-TIEN

Locality	District	Mineral
Niu Hsin T'ai	Pen-hsi	Coal
Tien Shih Fu Kou	Pen-hsi	Coal
Sha Sung Kang	Hai-lung	Coal
T'ieh Ch'ang	Tung-hua	Coal
Nuan Ti Tang	Chin	Coal

An Shan Chan region   From Liao-yang to Pen-
hsi .... Iron

PROVINCE OF KIRIN
(Southern Portion)

Sha Sung Kang	Ho-lung	Coal and Iron
Kang Yao	Chi-lin (Kirin)	Coal
Chia P'i Kou	Hua-tien	Gold

Art. 5. (Changed to an exchange of notes.)

The Chinese Government declares that China will hereafter provide funds for building railways in South Manchuria; if foreign capital is required, the Chinese Government agrees to negotiate for the loan with Japanese capitalists first.

Art. 5-a. (Changed to an exchange of notes.)

The Chinese Government agrees that hereafter, when a foreign loan is to be made on the security of the taxes of South Manchuria (not including customs and salt revenue on the security of which loans have already been made by the Central Government), it will negotiate for the loan with Japanese capitalists first.

Art. 6. (Changed to an exchange of notes.)

The Chinese Government declares that hereafter if foreign advisers or instructors on political, financial, military or police matters, are to be employed in South Manchuria, Japanese will be employed first.

Art. 7. The Chinese Government agree speedily to make a fundamental revision of the Kirin-Chang-chun Railway Loan Agreement, taking as a standard the provisions in railroad loan agreements made heretofore between China and foreign financiers. If, in future, more advantageous terms than those in existing railway loan agreements are granted to foreign financiers, in connection with railway loans, the above agreement shall again be revised in accordance with Japan's wishes.

All existing treaties between China and Japan relating to Manchuria shall, except where otherwise provided for by this Convention, remain in force.

1. The Chinese Government agrees that hereafter when a foreign loan is to be made on the security of the taxes of Eastern Inner Mongolia, China must negotiate with the Japanese Government first.

2. The Chinese Government agrees that China will herself provide funds for building the railways in Easttern Inner Mongolia; if foreign capital is required, she must negotiate with the Japanese Government first.

3. The Chinese Government agrees, in the interest of trade and for the residence of foreigners, to open by China herself, as soon as possible, certain suitable places in Eastern Inner Mongolia as Commercial Ports. The places which ought to be opened are to be chosen, and the regulations are to be drafted, by the Chinese Government, but the Japanese Minister must be consulted before making a decision.

4. In the event of Japanese and Chinese desiring jointly to undertake agricultural enterprises and industries incidental thereto, the Chinese Government shall give its permission.

GROUP III

The relations between Japan and the Hanyehping Company being very intimate, if those interested in the said Company come to an agreement with the Japanese capitalists for co-operation, the Chinese Government shall forthwith give its consent thereto. The Chinese Government further agrees that, without the consent of the Japanese capitalists, China will not convert the Company into a state enterprise, nor confiscate it, nor cause it to borrow and use foreign capital other than Japanese.

GROUP IV

China is to give pronouncement by herself in accordance with the following principle:

No bay, harbour, or island along the coast of China may be ceded or leased to any Power.

Notes to be exchanged.

A

As regards the right of financing a railway from Wuchang to connect with the Kiu-kiang-Nanchang line, the Nanchang-Hangchow railway, and the Nanchang-Chaochow railway, if it is clearly ascertained that other Powers have no objection, China shall grant the said right to Japan.

B

As regards the rights of financing a railway from Wuchang to connect with the Kiu-kiang-Nanchang railway, a railway from Nanchang to Hangchow and

another from Nanchang to Chaochow, the Chinese
Government shall not grant the said right to any
foreign Power before Japan comes to an understanding with the other Power which is heretofore interested therein.

NOTES TO BE EXCHANGED

The Chinese Government agrees that no nation whatever is to be permitted to construct, on the coast of
Fukien Province, a dockyard, a coaling station for
military use, or a naval base; nor to be authorized
to set up any other military establishment. The Chinese Government further agrees not to use foreign
capital for setting up the above mentioned construction or establishment.

Mr. Lu, the Minister of Foreign Affairs, stated as
follows:

1. The Chinese Government shall, whenever, in future, it considers this step necessary, engage numerous
Japanese advisers.

2. Whenever, in future, Japanese subjects desire
to lease or purchase land in the interior of China for
establishing schools or hospitals, the Chinese Government shall forthwith give its consent thereto.

3. When a suitable opportunity arises in future,
the Chinese Government will send military officers to
Japan to negotiate with Japanese military authorities
the matter of purchasing arms or that of establishing
a joint arsenal.

Mr. Hioki, the Japanese Minister, stated as follows:

As relates to the question of the right of missionary propaganda the same shall be taken up again for negotiation in future.

(B) CHINA'S REPLY TO JAPAN'S REVISED DEMANDS

China's Reply of May 1, 1915, to the Japanese Revised Demands of April 26, 1915.

GROUP I

The Chinese Government and the Japanese Government, being desirous of maintaining the general peace in Eastern Asia and further strengthening the friendly relations and good neighbourhood existing between the two nations, agree to the following articles:

Article 1. The Chinese Government declare that they will give full assent to all matters upon which the Japanese and German Governments may hereafter mutually agree, relating to the disposition of all interests which Germany, by virtue of treaties or recorded cases, possesses in relation to the Province of Shantung.

The Japanese Government declares that when the Chinese Government give their assent to the disposition of interests above referred to, Japan will restore the leased territory of Kiaochow to China; and further recognize the right of the Chinese Government to participate in the negotiations referred to above between Japan and Germany.

Article 2. The Japanese Government consent to be responsible for the indemnification of all losses occasioned by Japan's military operation around the leased territory of Kiaochow shall, prior to the restoration of the said leased territory to China, be administered as heretofore, for the time being. The railways and telegraph lines erected by Japan for military purposes are to be removed forthwith. The Japanese troops now stationed outside the original leased territory of Kiaochow are now to be withdrawn first, those within the original leased territory are to be withdrawn on the restoration of the said leased territory to China.

Article 3. (Changed into an exchange of notes.)

The Chinese Government declare that within the Province of Shantung and along its coast no territory or island will be ceded or leased to any Power under any pretext.

Article 4. The Chinese Government consent that as regards the railway to be built by China herself from Chefoo or Lungkow to connect with the Kiaochow-Tsinanfu Railway, if Germany is willing to abandon the privilege of financing the Che-foo-Weihsien line, China will approach Japanese capitalists for a loan.

Article 5. The Chinese Government engage, in the interest of trade and for the residence of foreigners, to open by herself as soon as possible certain suitable places in the Province of Shantung as Commercial Ports.

(Supplementary exchange of notes.)

The places which ought to be opened are to be chosen, and the regulations are to be drafted, by the

Chinese Government, but the Japanese Minister must be consulted before making a decision.

Article 6. If the Japanese and German Governments are not able to come to a definite agreement in future in their negotiations respecting transfer, etc., this provisional agreement contained in the foregoing articles shall be void.

Group II

The six articles which are found in Japan's Revised Demands of April 26, 1915, but omitted herein, are those already initialed by the Chinese Foreign Minister and the Japanese Minister.

The Chinese Government and the Japanese Government, with a view to developing their economic relations in South Manchuria, agree to the following articles:

Article 2. Japanese subjects in South Manchuria may, by arrangement with the owners, lease land required for erecting suitable buildings for trade and manufacture or for agricultural enterprises.

Article 3. Japanese subjects shall be free to reside and travel in South Manchuria and to engage in business and manufacture of any kind whatsoever.

Article 3 a. The Japanese subjects referred to in the preceding two articles, besides being required to register with the local authorities passports, which they must procure under the existing regulations, shall also observe police rules and regulations and pay taxes in the same manner as Chinese. Civil and criminal cases shall be tried and adjudicated by the authorities of the defendant's nationality and an officer can be deputed to attend the proceedings. But all cases purely between Japanese subjects, and mixed cases between Japanese and Chinese, relating to land or disputes arising from lease contracts, shall be tried and adjudicated by Chinese Authorities and the Japanese Consul may also depute an officer to attend the proceedings.

When the judicial system in the said Province is completely reformed, all the civil and criminal cases concerning Japanese subjects shall be tried entirely by Chinese law courts.

RELATING TO EASTERN INNER MONGOLIA
(To be exchanged by notes)

Article 1. The Chinese Government declare that China will not in future pledge the taxes, other than customs and salt revenue, of that part of Eastern Inner Mongolia under the jurisdiction of South Manchuria and Jehol Intendency, as security for raising loans.

Article 2. The Chinese Government declare that China will herself provide funds for building the railways in that part of Eastern Inner Mongolia under the jurisdiction of South Manchuria and the Jehol Intendency; if foreign capital is required, China will negotiate with Japanese capitalists first, provided this does not conflict with agreements already concluded with other Powers.

Article 3. The Chinese Government agrees, in the interest of trade and for the residence of foreigners, to open by China herself certain suitable places in that part of Eastern Inner Mongolia under the jurisdiction of South Manchuria and the Jehol Intendency, as Commercial Marts.

The regulations for the said Commercial Marts will be made in accordance with those of other Commercial Marts opened by China herself.

GROUP III

The relations between Japan and the Hanyehping Company being very intimate, if the said Company comes to an agreement with the Japanese capitalists for co-operation, the Chinese Government shall forthwith give their consent thereto. The Chinese Government further declare that China will not convert the Company into a state enterprise, nor confiscate it nor cause it to borrow and use foreign capital other than Japanese.

Letter to be Addressed by the Japanese Minister to the Chinese Minister of Foreign Affairs

Excellency:

I have the honour to state that a report has reached me that the Chinese Government have given permission to foreign nations to construct on the coast of Fukien Province dock-yards, coaling stations for military use, naval bases and other establishments for military purposes and further that the Chinese Government are borrowing foreign capital for putting up the above-mentioned construction or establishments. I shall be much obliged if the Chinese Government will inform me whether ⟩r not these reports are well founded in fact.

Reply to be Addressed by the Chinese Minister of Foreign Affairs to the Japanese Minister

Excellency:

I have the honour to acknowledge the receipt of your Excellency's Note of ―― ――. In reply I beg to state that the Chinese Government have not given permission to foreign Powers to construct, on the coast of Fukien Province, dock-yards, coaling stations for military use, naval bases or other establishments for military purposes; nor do they contemplate borrowing foreign capital for putting up such constructions or establishments.

(C) MEMORANDUM READ BY THE MINISTER OF FOREIGN AFFAIRS TO MR. HICKI, THE JAPANESE MINISTER, AT A CONFERENCE HELD AT WAICHIAOPU, MAY I, 1915

The list of demands which the Japanese Government first presented to the Chinese Government consists of five groups, the first relating to Shantung, the second relating to South Manchuria and Eastern Inner Mongolia, the third relating to the Hanyehping Company, the fourth asking for non-alienation of the coast of the country, and the fifth relating to the questions of national advisers, national police, national arms, missionary propaganda, Yangtze Valley railways, and Fukien Province. Out of profound regard for the intentions entertained by Japan, the Chinese Government took these momentous demands into grave and careful consideration and decided to negotiate with the Japanese Government frankly and sincerely what were possible to negotiate. This is a manifestation to Japan of the most profound regard which the Chinese Government entertains for the relations between the two nations.

Ever since the opening of the negotiations China has been doing her best to hasten their progress, holding as many as three conferences a week. As regards the articles in the second group, the Chinese Government, being disposed to allow the Japanese Government to develop the economic relations of the two countries in South Manchuria, realizing that the Japanese Government attaches importance to its interests in that region, and wishing to meet the hopes of Japan, made a painful effort, without hesitation, to agree to the extension of the 25-year lease of Port Arthur and Dalny, the 36-year period of the South Manchuria railway and the 15-year period of the Antung-Mukden railway, all to 99 years; and to abandon its own cherished hopes to regain control of these places and properties at the expiration of their respective original terms of lease. It cannot but be admitted that this is a most genuine proof of China's friendship for Japan. As to the rights of opening mines in South Manchuria, the Chinese Government has already agreed to permit Japanese to work mines within the mining areas designated by Japan. China has further agreed to give Japan a right of preference in the event of borrowing foreign capital for building railways or of making a loan on the security of the local taxes in South Manchuria. The question of revising the arrangement for the Kirin-Changchun railway has been settled in accordance with the proposal made by Japan. The Chinese Government has further agreed to employ Japanese first in the event of employing foreign advisers on political, military, financial and police matters.

Furthermore, the provision about the repurchase period in the South Manchurian railway was not mentioned in Japan's original proposal. Subsequently, the Japanese Government alleging that its meaning was not clear, asked China to cancel the provision altogether. Again, Japan at first demanded the right of Japanese to carry on farming in South Manchuria, but subsequently she considered the word " farming " was not broad enough and asked to replace it with the phrase " agricultural enterprises." To these requests the Chinese Government, though well aware that the proposed changes could only benefit Japan, still acceded without delay. This, too, is a proof of China's frankness and sincerity toward Japan.

As regards matters relating to Shantung, the Chinese Government has agreed to a majority of the demands.

The question of inland residence in South Manchuria is, in the opinion of the Chinese Government, incompatible with the treaties China has entered into with Japan and other Powers, still the Chinese Government did its best to consider how it was possible to avoid that incompatibility. At first, China suggested that the Chinese Authorities should have full rights of jurisdiction over Japanese settlers. Japan declined to agree to it. Thereupon China reconsidered the question and revised her counter-proposal five or six times, each time making some definite concession, and went so far as to agree that all civil and criminal cases between Chinese and Japanese should be arranged according to existing treaties. Only cases relating to land or lease contracts were reserved to be adjudicated by Chinese Courts, as a mark of China's sovereignty over the region. This is another proof of China's readiness to concede as much as possible.

Eastern Inner Mongolia is not an enlightened region as yet and the conditions existing there are entirely different from those prevailing in South Manchuria. The two places, therefore, cannot be considered in the same light. Accordingly, China agreed to open commercial marts first, in the interests of foreign trade.

The Hanyehping Company mentioned in the third group is entirely a private company, and the Chinese Government is precluded from interfering with it and negotiating with another government to make any disposal of the same as the Government likes, but having regard for the interests of the Japanese capitalists, the Chinese Government agreed that whenever, in future, the said company and the Japanese capitalists should arrive at a satisfactory arrangement for co-operation, China will give her assent thereto. Thus the interests of the Japanese capitalists are amply safeguarded.

Although the demand in the fourth group asking for a declaration not to alienate China's coast is an infringement of her sovereign rights, yet the Chinese Government offered to make a voluntary pronouncement so far as it comports with China's sovereign rights. Thus, it is seen that the Chinese Government, in deference to the wishes of Japan, gave a most serious consideration even to those demands which gravely affect the sovereignty and territorial rights of China as well as the principle of equal opportunity and the treaties with foreign Powers. All this was a painful effort on the part of the Chinese Government to meet the situation — a fact of which the Japanese Government must be aware.

As regards the demands in the fifth group, they all infringe China's sovereignty, the treaty rights of other Powers or the principle of equal opportunity. Although Japan did not indicate any difference between this group and the preceding four in the list which she presented to China in respect of their character, the Chinese Government, in view of their palpably objectionable features, persuaded itself that these could not have been intended by Japan as anything other than Japan's mere advice to China. Accordingly

China has declared from the very beginning that while she entertains the most profound regard for Japan's wishes, she was unable to admit that any of these matters could be made the subject of an understanding with Japan. Much as she desired to pay regard to Japan's wishes, China cannot but respect her own sovereign rights and the existing treaties with other Powers. In order to be rid of the seed for future misunderstanding and to strengthen the basis of friendship, China was constrained to iterate the reasons for refusing to negotiate on any of the articles in the fifth group, yet in view of Japan's wishes China has expressed her readiness to state that no foreign money was borrowed to construct harbour works in Fukien Province. Thus it is clear that China went so far as to seek a solution for Japan of a question that really did not admit of negotiation. Was there, then, evasion on the part of China?

Now, since the Japanese Government has presented a revised list of demands and declared at the same time that it will restore the leased territory of Kiaochow, the Chinese Government reconsiders the whole question and herewith submits a new reply to the friendly Japanese Government.

In this reply the unsettled articles in the first group are stated again for discussion. As regards the second group, those articles which have already been initialed are omitted. In connection with the question of inland residence the police regulation clause has been revised in a more restrictive sense. As for the trial of cases relating to land and lease contracts the Chinese Government now permits the Japanese Consul to send an officer to attend the proceedings. Of the four demands in connection with that part of Eastern Inner Mongolia which is within the jurisdiction of South Manchuria and the Jehol Intendency, China agrees to three. China, also, agrees to the article relating to the Hanyehping Company as revised by Japan.

It is hoped that the Japanese Government will appreciate the conciliatory spirit of the Chinese Government in making this final concession and forthwith give her assent thereto.

There is one more point. At the beginning of the present negotiations it was mutually agreed to observe secrecy, but unfortunately a few days after the presentation of the demands by Japan an Osaka newspaper published an " Extra " giving the text of the demands. The foreign and the Chinese press has since been paying considerable attention to this question and frequently publishing pro-Chinese or pro-Japanese comments in order to call forth the world's conjecture, a matter which the Chinese Government deeply regrets. The Chinese Government has never carried on any newspaper campaign and the Chinese Minister of Foreign Affairs has repeatedly declared it to the Japanese Minister.

In conclusion, the Chinese Government wishes to express its hope that the negotiations now pending between the two countries will soon come to an end and

whatever misgivings foreign countries entertain toward the present situation may be quickly dispelled.

(D) JAPAN'S ULTIMATUM TO CHINA

Japan's Ultimatum delivered by the Japanese Minister to the Chinese Government, on May 7th, 1915.

The reason why the Imperial Government opened
the present negotiations with the Chinese Government
is first to endeavour to dispose of the complications
arising out of the war between Japan and China,
and secondly to attempt to solve those various questions which are detrimental to the intimate relations
of China and Japan with a view to solidifying the
foundation of cordial friendship subsisting between
the two countries to the end that the peace of the Far
East may be effectually and permanently preserved.
With this object in view, definite proposals were presented to the Chinese Government in January of this
year, and up to today as many as twenty-five conferences have been held with the Chinese Government in
perfect sincerity and frankness.

In the course of negotiations the Imperial Government have consistently explained the aims and objects
of the proposals in a conciliatory spirit, while on the
other hand the proposals of the Chinese Government,
whether important or unimportant, have been attended to without any reserve.

It may be stated with confidence that no effort
has been spared to arrive at a satisfactory and amicable
settlement of those questions.

The discussion of the entire corpus of the proposals was practically at an end at the twenty-fourth conference; that is on the 17th of the last month. The Imperial Government, taking a broad view of the negotiation and in consideration of the points raised by the Chinese Government, modified the original proposals with considerable concessions and presented to the Chinese Government on the 26th of the same month the revised proposals for agreement, and at the same time it was offered that, on the acceptance of the revised proposals, the Imperial Government would, at a suitable opportunity, restore, with fair and proper conditions, to the Chinese Government the Kiaochow territory, in the acquisition of which the Imperial Government had made a great sacrifice.

On the first of May, the Chinese Government delivered the reply to the revised proposals of the Japanese Government, which is contrary to the expectations of the Imperial Government. The Chinese Government not only did not give a careful consideration to the revised proposals but even with regard to the offer of the Japanese Government to restore Kiaochow to the Chinese Government the latter did not manifest the least appreciation for Japan's good will and difficulties.

From the commercial and military point of view Kiaochow is an important place, in the acquisition of which the Japanese Empire sacrificed much blood and money, and, after the acquisition the Empire incurs no obligation to restore it to China. But with the ob-

ject of increasing the future friendly relations of
the two countries, they went to the extent of proposing
its restoration, yet to her great regret, the Chinese
Government did not take into consideration the good
intention of Japan and manifest appreciation of her
difficulties. Furthermore, the Chinese Government
not only ignored the friendly feelings of the Imperial
Government in offering the restoration of Kiaochow
Bay, but also in replying to the revised proposals they
even demanded its unconditional restoration; and
again China demanded that Japan should bear the responsibility of paying indemnity for all the unavoidable losses and damages resulting from Japan's military operations at Kiaochow; and still further in connection with the territory of Kiaochow China advanced other demands and declared that she has the
right of participation at the future peace conference
to be held between Japan and Germany. Although
China is fully aware that the unconditional restoration of Kiaochow and Japan's responsibility of indemnification for the unavoidable losses and damages
can never be tolerated by Japan, yet she purposely
advanced these demands and declared that this reply
was final and decisive.

Since Japan could not tolerate such demands the
settlement of the other questions, however compromising it may be, would not be to her interest. The consequence is that the present reply of the Chinese Government is, on the whole, vague and meaningless.

Furthermore, in the reply of the Chinese Government to the other proposals in the revised list of the Imperial Government, such as South Manchuria and Eastern Inner Mongolia, where Japan particularly has geographical, commercial, industrial and strategic relations, as recognized by all nations, and made more remarkable in consequence of the two wars in which Japan was engaged, the Chinese Government overlooks these facts and does not respect Japan's position in that place. The Chinese Government even freely altered those articles which the Imperial Government, in a compromising spirit, have formulated in accordance with the statement of the Chinese Representatives, thereby making the statements of the Representatives an empty talk; and on seeing them conceding with the one hand and withholding with the other it is very difficult to attribute faithfulness and sincerity to the Chinese authorities.

As regards the articles relating to the employment of advisers, the establishment of schools and hospitals, the supply of arms and ammunition and the establishment of arsenals and railway concessions in South China in the revised proposals, they were either proposed with the proviso that the consent of the Power concerned must be obtained, or they are merely to be recorded in the minutes in accordance with the statements of the Chinese delegates, and thus they are not in the least in conflict either with Chinese sovereignty or her treaties with the Foreign Powers, yet the Chinese Government in their reply to the proposals, alleging that these proposals are incompatible with their sovereign rights and treaties with Foreign Powers, defeat the expectations of the Imperial Government. However, in spite of such attitude of the Chinese Government, the Imperial Government, though regretting to see that there is no room for further negotiations, yet warmly attached to the preservation of the peace of the Far East, is still hoping for a satisfactory settlement in order to avoid the disturbance of the relations.

So in spite of the circumstances which admitted no patience, they have reconsidered the feelings of the Government of their neighbouring country and, with the exception of the article relating to Fukien which is to be the subject of an exchange of notes as has already been agreed upon by the Representatives of both nations, will undertake to detach the Group V from the present negotiations and discuss it separately in the future. Therefore, the Chinese Government should appreciate the friendly feelings of the Imperial Government by immediately accepting without any alteration all the articles of Groups I, II, III, and IV and the exchange of notes in connection with Fukien province in Group V as contained in the revised proposals presented on the 26th of April.

The Imperial Government hereby again offer their advice and hope that the Chinese Government, upon this advice, will give a satisfactory reply by 6 o'clock P. M. on the 9th day of May. It is hereby declared that if no satisfactory reply is received before or at the specified time, the Imperial Government will take steps they may deem necessary.

EXPLANATORY NOTE

Accompanying Ultimatum delivered to the Minister of Foreign Affairs by the Japanese Minister, May 7th, 1915.

1. With the exception of the question of Fukien to be arranged by an exchange of notes, the five articles postponed for later negotiation refer to (a) the employment of advisers, (b) the establishment of schools and hospitals, (c) the railway concessions in South China, (d) the supply of arms and ammunition and the establishment of arsenals and (e) right of missionary propaganda.

2. The acceptance by the Chinese Government of the article relating to Fukien may be either in the form as proposed by the Japanese Minister on the 26th of April or in that contained in the Reply of the Chinese Government of May 1st. Although the Ultimatum calls for the immediate acceptance by China of the modified proposals presented on April 26th, without alteration, but it should be noted that it merely states the principle and does not apply to this article and articles 4 and 5 of this note.

3. If the Chinese Government accept all the articles as demanded in the Ultimatum the offer of the Japanese Government to restore Kiaochow to China, made on the 26th of April, will still hold good.

purchase of land, the terms "lease" and "purchase" may be replaced by the terms "temporary lease" and "perpetual lease" or "lease on consultation," which means a long-term lease with its unconditional renewal.

Article IV of Group II relating to the approval of police laws and Ordinances and local taxes by the Japanese Council may form the subject of a secret agreement.

5. The phrase "to consult with the Japanese Government" in connection with questions of pledging the local taxes for raising loans and the loans for the construction of railways, in Eastern Inner Mongolia, which is similar to the agreement in Manchuria relating to the matters of the same kind, may be replaced by the phrase "to consult with the Japanese capitalists."

The article relating to the opening of trade marts in Eastern Inner Mongolia in respect to location and regulations, may, following their precedent set in Shantung, be the subject of an exchange of notes.

6. From the phrase "those interested in the Company" in Group III of the revised list of demands, the words "those interested in" may be deleted.

7. The Japanese version of the Formal Agreement and its annexes shall be the official text or both the Chinese and Japanese shall be the official texts.

(E) REPLY OF THE CHINESE GOVERNMENT TO THE ULTIMATUM OF THE JAPANESE GOVERNMENT,

DELIVERED TO THE JAPANESE MINISTER BY THE
MINISTER OF FOREIGN AFFAIRS ON THE 8TH OF
MAY, 1915

" On the 7th of this month, at three o'clock P. M.,
the Chinese Government received an Ultimatum from
the Japanese Government together with an Explanatory Note of seven articles. The Ultimatum concluded with the hope that the Chinese Government by
six o'clock P. M. on the 9th of May will give a satisfactory reply, and it is hereby declared that if no satisfactory reply is received before or at the specified
time, the Japanese Government will take steps she
may deem necessary.

" The Chinese Government with a view to preserving
the peace of the Far East hereby accepts, with the exception of those five articles of Group V postponed
for later negotiations, all the articles of Groups I, II,
III, and IV and the exchange of notes in connection
with Fukien Province in Group V as contained in the
revised proposals presented on the 26th of April,
and in accordance with the Explanatory Note of seven
articles accompanying the Ultimatum of the Japanese
Government with the hope that thereby all the out-
standing questions are settled, so that the cordial relationship between the two countries may be further consolidated.   The Japanese Minister is hereby requested
to appoint a day to call at the Ministry of Foreign Affairs to make the literary improvement of the text
and sign the Agreement as soon as possible."

(F) EXTRACT FROM OFFICIAL STATEMENT ISSUED BY
THE CHINESE GOVERNMENT AFTER THE ACCEPT-
ANCE OF THE JAPANESE ULTIMATUM, MAY 8TH,
1915

" In considering the nature of the course they should take with reference to the Ultimatum the Chinese Government was influenced by a desire to preserve the Chinese people, as well as the large number of foreign residents in China, from unnecessary suffering, and also to prevent the interests of friendly Powers from being imperiled. For these reasons the Chinese Government were constrained to comply in full with the terms of the Ultimatum, but in complying the Chinese disclaim any desire to associate themselves with any revision, which may thus be effected, of the various conventions and agreements concluded between other Powers in respect of the maintenance of China's territorial independence and integrity, the preservation of the status quo, and the principle of equal opportunity for the commerce and industry of all nations in China." [1]

[1] For the full text of this statement, see *Our Eastern Question*, by T. F. Millard. The texts of the treaties concluded between China and Japan as a result of the Twenty-one Demands is contained in that volume, and also in *Contemporary Politics in the Far East* by S. K. Hornbeck; and *The Fight for the Republic in China*, by B. L. Putnam-Weale.

APPENDIX III

OFFICIAL STATEMENTS IN RELATION TO THE LAN-
SING-ISHII AGREEMENT BETWEEN AMERICA
AND JAPAN CONCERNING CHINA, IN 1917.

(A) STATEMENT BY SECRETARY LANSING AFTER
PUBLICATION OF THE ISHII AGREEMENT

"Viscount Ishii and the other Japanese commissioners who are now on their way back to their country have performed a service to the United States
as well as to Japan which is of the highest value.

"There had unquestionably been growing up between the peoples of the two countries a feeling of
suspicion as to the motives inducing the activities of
the other in the Far East, a feeling which, if unchecked,
promised to develop a serious situation. Rumours
and reports of improper intentions were increasing and
were more and more believed. Legitimate commercial and industrial enterprises without ulterior motive
were presumed to have political significance, with the
result that opposition to those enterprises were aroused
in the other country.

"The attitude of constraint and doubt thus created
was fostered and encouraged by the campaign of
falsehood, which for a long time had been adroitly
and secretly carried on by Germans, whose government,
as a part of its foreign policy, desired especially to
so alienate this country and Japan that it would be
at the chosen time no difficult task to cause a rupture

of their good relations. Unfortunately, there were people in both countries, many of whom were entirely honest in their beliefs, who accepted every false rumour as true, and aided the German propaganda by declaring that their own government should prepare for the conflict, which, they asserted, was inevitable, that the interests of the two nations in the Far East were hostile, and that every activity of the other country in the Pacific had a sinister purpose.

" Fortunately, this distrust was not so general in either the United States or Japan as to affect the friendly relations of the two governments, but there is no doubt that the feeling of suspicion was increasing, and the untrue reports were receiving more and more credence in spite of the earnest efforts which were made on both sides of the Pacific to counteract a movement which would jeopardize the ancient friendship of the two nations.

" The visit of Viscount Ishii and his colleagues has accomplished a great change of opinion in this country. By frankly denouncing the evil influences which have been at work, by openly proclaiming that the policy of Japan is not one of aggression, and by declaring that there is no intention to take advantage commercially or industrially of the special relations to China created by geographical position, the representatives of Japan have cleared the diplomatic atmosphere of the suspicions which had been so carefully spread by our enemies and by misguided or overzealous people in both countries. In a few days the propaganda of years has been undone, and both nations are now able to see how near they came to being led into the trap which had been skilfully set for them.

" Throughout the conferences which have taken place, Viscount Ishii has shown a sincerity and candour which dispelled every doubt as to his purpose, and brought the two governments into an attitude of confidence toward each other which made it possible to discuss every question with frankness and cordiality. Approaching the subjects in such a spirit and with the mutual desire to remove every possible cause of controversy, the negotiations were marked by a sincerity and good will which from the first ensured their success.

" The principal result of the negotiations was the mutual understanding which was reached as to the principles governing the policies of the two governments in relation to China. This understanding is formally set forth in the notes exchanged, and now made public. The statements in the notes require no explanation. They not only contain a reaffirmation of the ' open door ' policy, but introduce a principle of non-interference with the sovereignty and territorial integrity of China which, generally applied, is essential to perpetual international peace, as clearly declared by President Wilson, and which is the very foundation, also, of Pan-Americanism, as interpreted by this government.

" The removal of doubts and suspicions and the mutual declaration of the new doctrine as to the Far

East would be enough to make the visit of the Japanese commission to the United States historic and memorable, but it accomplished a further purpose, which is of special interest to the world at this time, in expressing Japan's earnest desire to co-operate with this country in waging war against the German government. The discussions, which covered the military, naval and economic activities to be employed with due regard to relative resources and ability, showed the sáme spirit of sincerity and candour which characterized the negotiations resulting in the exchange of notes.

"At the present time it is inexpedient to make public the details of these conversations, but it may be said that this government has been gratified by the assertions of Viscount Ishii and his colleagues that their government desired to do their part in the suppression of Prussian militarism and were eager to co-operate in every practical way to that end. It might be added, however, that complete and satisfactory understandings upon the matter of naval co-operation in the Pacific for the purpose of attaining the common object against Germany and her allies have been reached between the representative of the imperial Japanese navy, who is attached to the special mission of Japan, and the representative of the United States Navy.

"It is only just to say that success which has attended the intercourse of the Japanese commission with American officials, and with private persons as well, is due in large measure to the personality of Viscount Ishii, the head of the mission. The natural reserve and hesitation, which are not unusual in negotiations of a delicate nature, disappeared under the influence of his open friendliness, while his frankness won the confidence and good will of all. It is doubtful if a representative of a different temper could in so short a time have done as much as Viscount Ishii to place on a better and firmer basis the relations between the United States and Japan. Through him the American people have gained a new and higher conception of the reality of Japan's friendship for the United States which will be mutually beneficial in the future.

" Viscount Ishii will be remembered in this country as a statesman of high attainments, as a diplomat with a true vision of international affairs, and as a genuine and outspoken friend of America."

(B) STATEMENT OF CHINESE GOVERNMENT CONCERNING THE LANSING-ISHII AGREEMENT

WASHINGTON, NOVEMBER 12, 1917

" The Government of the United States and the Government of Japan have recently, in order to silence mischievous reports, effected an exchange of notes at Washington concerning their desires and intentions with regard to China. Copies of the said notes have been communicated to the Chinese Government by the Japanese Minister at Peking, and the Chinese Government, in order to avoid misunderstanding, hastens to make the following declaration so as to make known the views of the Government.

" The principle adopted by the Chinese Government toward the friendly nations has always been one of justice and equality, and consequently the rights enjoyed by the friendly nations derived from the treaties have been constantly respected, and so even with the special relations between countries created by the fact of territorial contiguity it is only in so far as they have already been provided for in her existing treaties.

" Hereafter the Chinese Government will still adhere to the principles hitherto adopted, and hereby it is again declared that the Chinese Government will not allow itself to be bound by any agreement entered into by other nations."

APPENDIX IV

TREATIES AND AGREEMENTS WITH REFERENCE
TO THE INTEGRITY AND SOVEREIGN RIGHTS
OF CHINA, THE "OPEN DOOR" POLICY
AND "EQUALITY OF OPPORTUNITIES"

I. Circular Note of Secretary of State John Hay, for the United States, sent on Sept. 6, 1899, to the diplomatic representatives of the United States at London, Paris, Berlin, and St. Petersburg, and in November to Rome and Tokyo, asking the governments of the countries to which they were respectively accredited to make a " formal declaration of an ' open door policy ' in the territories held by them in China."

The request made of each government was that it:

" First. Will in no way interfere with any treaty port or any vested interest within any so-called ' sphere of interest ' or leased territory it may have in China.

" Second. That the Chinese treaty tariff of the time being shall apply to all merchandise landed or shipped to all such ports . . . (unless they be ' free ports '), . . . and that duties so leviable shall be collected by the Chinese Government.

" Third. That it will levy no higher harbour dues on vessels of another nationality frequenting any port in such ' sphere ' than shall be levied on vessels of its own nationality, and no higher railroad charges

over lines built, controlled, or operated within its
'sphere' on merchandise belonging to citizens or subjects of other nationalities transported through such
'sphere' than shall be levied on similar merchandise
belonging to its own nationals transported over equal
distances."

Each of the governments so addressed gave its assent
to the principles suggested, whereupon Secretary Hay,
having in hand and having compared the replies, sent,
on March 20, 1900, instructions mutatis mutandis, to
the ambassadors to inform the governments to which
they were respectively accredited that in his opinion the
six powers in question and the United States were mutually pledged to the policy of maintaining the commercial status quo in China, and of refraining each within
what might be considered its " sphere of influence "
from measures "calculated to destroy equality of
opportunity." The seven powers thus mutually
pledged were France, Germany, Great Britain, Italy,
Japan, Russia, and the United States. (The United
States had, however, no special " sphere of influence.")

II. Circular Telegram sent by Mr. Hay to the
diplomatic representatives of the United States at
Berlin, Brussels, The Hague, Lisbon, London, Madrid,
Paris, Rome, St. Petersburg, Tokyo, and Vienna, July
3, 1900.

" . . . the policy of the Government of the United
States is to seek a solution which may bring about
permanent safety and peace to China, preserve China's
territorial and administrative entity, protect all rights

guaranteed to friendly powers by treaty and international laws, and safeguard for the world the principle of equal and impartial trade with all parts of the Chinese Empire."

III. Lord Salisbury, English Prime Minister, in an interview with the United States Ambassador to England, July 7, 1900, " expressed himself most emphatically as concurring " in the policy of the United States as set forth in the above telegram.

In a statement made in the English House of Commons, Aug. 2, 1900, regarding the policy of the British Government, it was declared:

" Her Majesty's Government are opposed to any partition of China, and believe that they are in accord with other powers in this declaration."

IV. Agreement, Great Britain-Germany — Oct. 16, 1900.

" 1. It is a matter of joint and permanent international interest that the ports on the rivers and the littoral of China should remain free and open to trade and to every other legitimate form of economic activity for the nationals of all countries without distinction, and the two agree on their part to uphold the same for all Chinese territory so far as they can exercise influence.

" 2. Her Britannic Majesty's Government and the Imperial German Government will not on their part make use of the present complication to obtain for themselves any territorial advantages in Chinese dominions and will direct their policy toward maintaining undiminished the territorial conditions of the Chinese Empire."

V. Mr. Hay, Oct. 29, 1900.

" When the recent troubles were at their height this government, on the 3d of July, once more made an announcement of its policy regarding impartial trade and the integrity of the Chinese Empire and had the gratification of learning that all the powers held similar views."

As the above Note indicates, the eleven countries addressed by Secretary Hay in his telegram of July 3 had all signified in one way or another their approval of the principles to which he asked attention in that telegram.

VI. For the Anglo-Japanese Treaty of Aug. 12, 1902, see Appendix V, under " Treaties . . . Korea," V.

VII. Mr. Hay to United States Ambassadors to Germany, Austria-Hungary, Belgium, France, Great Britain, Italy, and Portugal, Jan. 13, 1905. (During the Russo-Japanese war.)

" . . . the United States has repeatedly made its position well known and has been gratified at the cordial welcome accorded to its efforts to strengthen and perpetuate the broad policy of maintaining the integrity of China and the ' open door ' in the Orient. . . . Holding these views, the United States disclaims any sort of reserved territorial rights or control in the Chinese Empire, and it is deemed fitting to make this purpose frankly known and to remove all apprehension on this score so far as concerns the policy of this nation. . . . You will bring this matter to the notice of the Government to which you are accredited, and you will invite the expression of its views thereon."

By Jan. 23 replies had been received from the Governments of Germany, Austria-Hungary, France, Great Britain, and Italy, entirely agreeing with the position taken by the United States and declaring their constant adhesion to the policy of the integrity of China and the open door in the Orient.

VIII. Treaty, Great Britain and Japan — Aug. 12, 1905. (Renewing the Alliance.)

Preamble. " The Governments of Great Britain and Japan . . . have agreed upon the following articles, which have for their objects:

" (a) The consolidation and maintainance of the general peace in the regions of Eastern Asia and of India.

" (b) The preservation of the common interests of all the powers in China by insuring the independence and the integrity of the Chinese Empire and the principle of equal opportunities for the commerce and industry of all nations in China."

For reference in this treaty to Korea, see Appendix V, under " Treaties . . . Korea," IX.

IX. Dispatch (Accompanying a copy of the foregoing) from the Marquis of Lansdowne to his Majesty's Minister at St. Petersburg, Sept. 6, 1905.

" Sir: I enclose . . . a copy of a new Agreement. . . . The Russian Government will, I trust, recognize that the new Agreement is an international instrument to which no exception can be taken by any of the powers interested in the affairs of the Far East. You should call special attention to the objects mentioned in the Preamble as those by which the policy of the contracting parties is inspired. His Majesty's Government believe that they may count upon the good will and support of all the powers in endeavouring to maintain peace in Eastern Asia and in seeking to uphold the integrity and independence of the Chinese Empire and the principle of equal opportunity for the commerce and the industry of all nations in that country."

X. Treaty (of Portsmouth), Russia-Japan — Sept. 5, 1905. (At the end of the Russo-Japanese War.)

Article 3. "Japan and Russia mutually engage . . . 2. To restore entirely and completely to the exclusive administration of China all portions of Manchuria now in the occupation or under the control of (their troops), with the exception of the territory above mentioned (the Liaotung peninsula).

"The Imperial Government of Russia declare that they have not in Manchuria any territorial advantage or exclusive concessions in impairment of Chinese sovereignty or inconsistent with the principle of equal opportunity."

Article 4. "Japan and Russia reciprocally engage not to obstruct any general measures common to all countries which China may take for the development of the commerce and industry of Manchuria."

XI. Treaty, China-Japan — Dec. 22, 1905.
(Confirming arrangements made in the Portsmouth Treaty.)

Article 12. The two governments " engage that in all matters dealt with in the treaty signed this day or in the present Agreement the most favourable treatment shall be reciprocally extended."

XII. Convention, France-Japan — June 10, 1907.

" The Governments of Japan and France, being agreed to respect the independence and integrity of China, as well as the principle of equal treatment in that country. . . ."

XIII. Convention, Japan-Russia — July 30, 1907.

Article 2. " The two High Contracting Parties recognize the independence and the territorial integrity of China and the principle of equal opportunity in whatever concerns the commerce and industry of all nations in that Empire, and engage to sustain and defend the status quo and respect for this principle by all the pacific means within their reach."

XIV. Exchange of Notes, Japan and the United States — November, 1908.

1. " It is the wish of the two Governments . . .

2. " They are also determined to preserve the common interests of all powers in China by supporting by all pacific means at their disposal the independence and the integrity of China and the principle of equal opportunity . . . in that Empire."

XV. Convention, Japan-Russia — July 4, 1910.

The two governments, " sincerely attached to the

principles established by the convention concluded between them on July 30, 1907, . . . "

Article 2. "Each . . . engages to maintain and respect the status quo in Manchuria resulting from the treaties, conventions and other arrangements concluded up to this day between Japan and Russia, or between either of those two Powers and China."

XVI. Treaty, Great Britain-Japan — July 13, 1911. (Renewing the alliance for the second time.)

Preamble: (The two governments declare as among their objects): "The preservation of the common interests of all Powers in China by insuring the independence and integrity of the Chinese Empire and the principle of equal opportunities for the commerce and industry of all nations in China."

XVII. Agreement, United States-Japan — Nov. 2, 1917.

"The Government of the United States recognizes that Japan has special interests in China, particularly in the parts to which her possessions are contiguous. . . . The territorial sovereignty of China, nevertheless, remains unimpaired . . . and the Japanese Government . . . has no desire to discriminate against the trade of other nations or to disregard the commercial rights heretofore granted by China in treaties with other Powers. The Government of the United States and Japan deny that they have any purpose to infringe in any way the independence or territorial integrity of China, and they declare furthermore, that

they always adhere to the principle of the so-called
' open door,' or equal opportunities for commerce and
industry in China."

With the exception of Clause XVII, this summary appears
in *Contemporary Politics in the Far East*, by S. K. Hornbeck,
copyrighted by D. Appleton & Co., and is here used by permission
of authors and publishers.

APPENDIX V

TREATIES AND AGREEMENTS WITH REFERENCE TO KOREA

I. Treaty, Japan-Korea — August 26, 1894. (At the beginning of the war between Japan and China.)
Article 1. "The object of the alliance is to maintain the independence of Korea on a firm footing and . . . "

II. Treaty (of Shimonoseki), Japan-China — April 17, 1895. (At the end of the war.)
Article 1. "China recognizes definitely the full and complete independence and autonomy of Korea."

III. Agreement, Japan-Russia — April 25, 1898.
Article 1. "The (two governments) recognize definitely the sovereignty and entire independence of Korea and pledge themselves mutually to abstain from all direct interference in the internal affairs of that country."

IV. Treaty, Korea-China — Sept. 11, 1899.
Article 1. "There shall be perpetual peace and friendship between the Empire of Korea and the Empire of China. . . . "

V. Treaty, England-Japan. (Making the Anglo-Japanese Alliance) — Jan. 30, 1902.
Preamble. "The Governments of Great Britain and Japan, actuated solely by a desire to maintain

the status quo and general peace in the Extreme East, being, moreover, specially interested in maintaining the territorial integrity of the Empire of China and the Empire of Korea, and in securing equal opportunities in those countries for the commerce and industry of all nations, hereby agree . . . "

Article 1. " The High Contracting Parties, having mutually recognized the independence of China and Korea, declare themselves to be entirely uninfluenced by any aggressive tendencies in either country."

VI. Convention, France-Russia — March 3, 1902.

The two governments " have received a copy of the Anglo-Japanese agreement of Jan. 30, 1902, concluded with the object of maintaining the status quo and the general peace in the Far East, and preserving the independence of China and Korea, which are to remain open to the commerce and industry of all nations . . .

" The two Governments consider that the observance of these principles is at the same time a guarantee of their special interests in the Far East."

VII. Rescript, by the Emperor of Japan, Feb. 10, 1904 (declaring war against Russia).

" . . .

" The integrity of Korea is a matter of gravest concern to this Empire, . . . the separate existence of Korea is essential to the safety of our realm.

" . . .

" . . . the absorption of Manchuria by Russia would render it impossible to maintain the integrity of China, and would, in addition, compel the abandonment of all hope for peace in the Extreme East . . . "

VIII. Protocol, Japan-Korea — Feb. 23, 1904.

Article 1. "For the purpose of maintaining a permanent and solid friendship between Japan and Korea and firmly establishing peace in the Far East, the Imperial Government of Korea shall place full confidence in the Imperial Government of Japan, and adopt the advice of the latter in regard to improvements in administration."

Article 2. "The Imperial Government of Japan shall in a spirit of firm friendship insure the safety and repose of the Imperial House of Korea."

Article 3. "The Imperial Government of Japan definitely guarantee the independence and territorial integrity of the Korean Empire."

IX. Treaty, Great Britain-Japan — August 12, 1905. (Renewing the Alliance.)

Article 3. "Japan possessing paramount political, military and economic interests in Korea, Great Britain recognizes the right of Japan to take such measures . . . in Korea as she may deem proper . . . provided that such measures are not contrary to the principle of equal opportunities for the commerce and industry of all nations."

X. Treaty (of Portsmouth), Japan-Russia — Sept. 5, 1905.

Article 2. "The Imperial Russian Government, acknowledging that Japan possesses in Korea paramount political, military, and economic interests, engage neither to obstruct nor to interfere with the measures . . . which the Imperial Japanese Government may find it necessary to take in Korea."

XI. Convention, Japan-Korea — Nov. 17, 1905.

Preamble. The two governments, "desiring to strengthen the principle of solidarity which unites the two Empires, have . . . concluded:

Article 1. "The Government of Japan . . . will hereafter have control and direction of the external relations and affairs of Korea . . . "

In 1906 Marquis Ito was made (Japanese) Resident-General in Korea.

In 1907 Japan prevented the representatives of the Korean Emperor from being given a hearing at The Hague Conference.

XII. Convention, Japan-Korea — July 24, 1907.

"The Governments of Japan and Korea, desiring speedily to promote the wealth and strength of Korea and with the object of promoting the prosperity of the Korean nation, have agreed. . . "

"1. In all matters relating to the reform of the Korean administration the Korean Government shall receive instructions and guidance from the (Japanese) Resident-General . . .

"4. In all appointments and removals of high officials the Korean Government must obtain the consent of the Resident-General.

"5. The Korean Government shall appoint to be officials of Korea any Japanese subjects recommended by the Resident-General.

" 6. The Korean Government shall not appoint any foreigners to be officials of Korea without consulting the Resident-General."

In 1908 Prince Ito declared publicly that it was no part of Japan's purpose to annex Korea.

In 1909 Prince Ito declared that Korea must be " amalgamated " with Japan.

XIII. Treaty, Japan-Korea — Aug. 22, 1910.

Article 1. " His Majesty the Emperor of Korea makes complete and permanent cession to his Majesty the Emperor of Japan of all rights of sovereignty over the whole of Korea."

Article 2. " His Majesty the Emperor of Japan accepts the cession mentioned in the preceding article, and consents to the complete annexation of Korea to the Empire of Japan."

On August 29, 1910, Japan formally declared Korea annexed to the dominions of his Imperial Majesty the Japanese Emperor.

(This summary appears in *Contemporary Politics in the Far East*, by S. K. Hornbeck, copyrighted by D. Appleton & Co., and is here used by permission of author and publishers.)

AN INTRODUCTORY BIBLIOGRAPHY
ON CHINA

(THE SO-CALLED "FIVE-FOOT SHELF" OF BOOKS
ON CHINA.)

The list of books given below, with one exception,[1] is that which was awarded the first-prize in a competition conducted in China for the selection of a limited list of the best books on China and its various phases of life and development. The competition was under the direction of an American periodical of the Orient, Millard's *Review of the Far East*, Shanghai, which announced several prizes for an "authoritative list of books which might serve as a foundation for a library dealing with all phases of Chinese life, art, trade, finance, customs, politics, international relations and history." Later this list was called a "five-foot shelf" of books on China. The competition was judged by Dr. Wu Ting-fang, former Chinese Minister to America, and Premier of China under President Li; Mr. Julean Arnold, American Commercial Attaché, American Legation, Peking; and Dr. F. L. Hawks-Pott, President of St. John's University of Shanghai. On Oct. 27, 1917, the following list sub-

---

[1] *Village Life in China,* by A. H. Smith, substituted for *Village and Town Life in China,* by Y. K. Leong and L. K. Tao.

mitted by the writer was awarded first prize. This list is obviously an introductory one; it could be easily expanded to twice its present proportions; on the other hand, it is difficult to reduce it without losing valuable information and a balanced perspective.

GENERAL AND INTRODUCTORY

1. *An Official Guide to Eastern Asia.* Vol IV. China: Imperial Japanese Government, Rwys., Tokio — 1915 Although inaccurate in certain respects, at present the best "Baedeker" of China.
2. *The Changing Chinese.* "The Conflict of Oriental and Western Cultures in China." E. A. Ross. Century Co., N. Y., 1912. A scientific, sociological view of China and its changes during the past decade. The East as it appears to the Western student.
3. *China: An Interpretation.* James W. Bashford. Abingdon Press, N. Y., 1916. A general view of present-day China by a competent observer and a missionary-statesman.
4. *The Middle Kingdom.* S. Wells Williams. 2 Vols. Chas. Scribner's Sons, N. Y., 1882. Revised edition, 1907. A standard work which still holds an authoritative place.

MANNERS AND CUSTOMS

5. *Chinese Characteristics.* A. H. Smith. Fleming H. Revell Co., N. Y. Fifteenth edition. First published, 1894. An interesting, though not very complimentary, description by a missionary author long resident in China.
6. *Village Life in China.* A. H. Smith. Fleming H. Revell Co., N. Y., 1899. A more detailed account of village customs by the same author. A standard work, which has passed the "thirteenth thousand" mark.

HISTORY

7. *The Ancient History of China, to the end of the Chou Dynasty, 249 B. C.* Frederich Hirth, Columbia Univ. Press, N. Y., 1908. Reprinted 1911. The best ancient history of China.
8. *A Sketch of Chinese History.* F. L. Hawks-Pott. Revised edition, 1915. Kelly & Walsh, Shanghai. The best condensed outline for an introductory study, for one familiar with Chinese names.
9. *Outlines of Chinese History.* Li Ung-bing. Commercial Press, Shanghai, 1914. A fuller treatment from the viewpoint of a Chinese writer; slightly inaccurate but interesting.
10. *China Under the Empress Dowager.* J. O. P. Bland and E. Backhouse. Wm. Heineman, London, 1910. Revised edition, 1914. A fascinating description of life in Peking before the days of the Republic, compiled from original documents. The authenticity of one of these documents has of late been questioned, but the book is nevertheless typical and of interest.

POLITICAL RELATIONS

11. *Intellectual and Political Currents in the Far East.* Paul S. Reinsch. Houghton Mifflin Co., N. Y., 1911. A balanced discussion of the subject by the present American Minister.
12. *Contemporary Politics in the Far East.* Stanley K. Hornbeck. D. Appleton & Co., N. Y., 1916. The clearest and fairest statement of the present situation.
13. *Our Eastern Question.* Thomas F. Millard. The Century Co., 1916. A strong argument concerning the present and future relations of China, Japan and America.

FINANCE

14. *The Trade and Administration of the Chinese Empire.* H. B. Morse. Longmans, Green & Co., N. Y., 1908. The best general work.

15. *The Gilds of China.* H. B. Morse. Longmans, Green & Co., London, 1909. A study of these particular organizations.
16. *The New Atlas and Commercial Gazetteer of China.* North China Daily News & Herald. Shanghai, 1917. "The biggest and best book on the resources of China" (*Millard's Review.*)

AGRICULTURE

17. *Farmers of Forty Centuries.* F. H. King. Macmillan Co., N. Y. Second edition. The most interesting and readable discussion of the subject.

PHYSIOGRAPHY AND GEOLOGY

18. *Letters of Baron Von Richthofen, 1902.* Shanghai. Containing the gist of his standard but untranslated work, *China.*

GEOGRAPHY

19. *Richard's Comprehensive Geography of the Chinese Empire.* Translated and revised by M. Kennelly, T'usewei Press. Shanghai, 1908.

TRAVEL

20. *A Yankee on the Yangtze.* W. E. Geil. A. C. Armstrong & Son, N. Y., 1904. A well written description of scenes and experiences on this great water-way.

RELIGION AND ETHICS

21. *The Three Religions of China.* W. E. Soothill. Hodder & Stoughton, London, 1913. Oxford lectures by a recognized authority. The best "popular" presentation of Buddhism, Taoism, Confucianism.
22. *The Religion of the Chinese.* J. J. M. de Groot. Macmillan, N. Y., 1910. Reprinted 1912. Lectures given at Hartford Seminary. A summary of the contents of his longer work, *The Religious Systems of China,* 6 volumes, 1892–1910. Emphasis on the animistic religion of the people rather than upon the "three religions" treated above.

23. *The Ethics of Confucius.* M. M. Dawson, with introduction by Wu Ting-fang. G. P. Putnam Sons, N. Y., 1915. Second impression. The sayings of Confucius and his disciples, arranged according to their original order, with commentary.

LITERATURE

24. *A History of Chinese Literature.* H. A. Giles. Wm. Heineman, London. D. Appleton, N. Y., 1901. "The first attempt in any language to produce a history of Chinese literature."

PHILOSOPHY

25. *Brief History of Early Chinese Philosophy.* D. T. Suzuki. Probsthain & Co., London 1914. A concise treatment by an Oriental scholar of high reputation.
26. *L'École Philosophique Moderne de la Chine.* Charles de Harlez. Vol. XLIX in Memoirs of the Belgian Academy of Sciences. The only description of the speculative philosophy of Chu Hi and the Sing-Li School.

MISSIONS

27. *The China Missions Year Book.* (Annual) Christian Literature Society, Shanghai. The most up-to-date and complete description of such work.

EDUCATION

28. *The Chinese System of Public Education.* P. W. Kuo. Originally a thesis written at Columbia University. Republished by Commercial Press, Shanghai, 1915. A sketch of the history and present-day problems of education in China.
29. *Educational Directory of China.* (Annual) Edward Evans & Sons, Shanghai. A manual of detailed information and statistics.

ART

30. *Chinese Art.* Stephen W. Bushell. Victoria and Albert Museum, London, 1904. Thrice reprinted. 2nd edition 1914. A general survey of the subject. A standard work.

31. *Chinese Pottery and Porcelain.* R. L. Hobson, 2 vols. Funk & Wagnalls, N. Y. Cassell & Co., London, 1913. Two volumes with handsome plates and pictures and the fullest and most detailed criticisms.

REFERENCE (GENERAL)

32. *The China Year Book.* (Annual) H. T. Montague Bell, & H. G. W. Woodhead. George Routledge Sons, London. E. P. Dutton & Co., N. Y. A valuable reference book.
33. *Encyclopedia Sinica.* Samuel Couling. Kelly & Walsh, Shanghai, 1917. A very valuable new work on "Things Chinese."

REFERENCE (CUSTOMS AND MANNERS)

34. *Researches into Chinese Superstitions.* Henry Doré. Translated by M. Kennelly. T'usewei Press, Shanghai. Thus far, 4 volumes, 1914–1918. The fullest and most accurate description of present customs and superstitions. Profusely illustrated.

REFERENCE (RELIGION AND LITERATURE)

35. *The Chinese Classics.* Original text and English translation by James Legge. 7 volumes. Oxford University Press, 2nd edition, 1893. "The introduction and commentary with the translation make this incomparably the most useful work in its field." (G. F. Moore.)

Three books have appeared since the compilation of this list which the author should like to add to it.

HISTORY

The Development of China. K. S. Latourette. Houghton Mifflin Co., N. Y., 1917. A concise, scholarly history of China, free from burdensome dates and details, with a final chapter on present-day problems and tendencies. The · best brief history for the student and general reader.

POLITICAL DEVELOPMENT

The Fight for the Republic in China. B. L. Putnam-Weale. Dodd, Mead & Co., N. Y., 1917. A detailed and optimistic account of the development of the Chinese Republic containing all the most important documents and data from 1911 to 1917. Indispensable for the student of that period.

DESCRIPTION IN VERSE

Profiles from China. Eunice Tietjens. Published by Ralph Fletcher Seymour, Chicago, 1917. A collection of sketches in free verse "of people and things seen in the interior." The familiar sights of China are pictured in striking and accurate phrase, in this "most unique volume of verse of the year."

INDEX

Administrative conference, 5.
Administrative council, 34.
America. See United States.
Analects, 47.
Anglo-Japanese Alliance, 8.
Annam, 103.
Assembly, national. See Parliament.
Assemblies, provincial. See Provincial self-government.
Atlas, steamship, 73.

Balkans, 147.
Bibliography on China, 252.
Black Dragon Memorandum, 12, 128, Appendix I.
Bolshevik, 144.
Boxer Indemnity, 86, 107, 152.
Boxer uprising, 107.
Boycott, against Japanese goods, 26.
British. See Great Britain.
Budget, 52.
Burlingame, Anson, 103.
Burma, 103.

Cabinet, Chinese, 45, 86, 87.
Cabinet, Japanese, 178.
Chang, Chinese Minister to Japan, 134 ff.
Chang, Hsun, 89, 94, 95 ff.
Chekiang, 50.
Chen, Eugene, 87, 129-130. See Peking Gazette.
Chengchiatung, 60 ff.

Chiang Chao-tsung, 94.
China Press, on China's severance of relations with Germany, 70-71; on Baron Ishii pledge, 124; on Sino-Japanese military agreement, 130-132.
Chou An Hui, 27, 32.
Christianity, 53-54.
Chuan Chao, 168, 169.
Cochin China, 103, 120.
Commerce, 161.
Concessions, 104.
Confucian Classics, 46.
Confucianism, 53-54.
Constitution, provisional, 3, 45; permanent, 48, 51, 54, 88, 89, 158.
Constitutional compact, 5.
Constitutional compact conference, 5.
Council of State, 5.
Currency, 160.
Customs duties, 80, 86, 104, 106, 107, 152, 169.
Czecho-Slovaks, 144.

Democracy in China, 26-28, 30 ff., 46, 47, 51, 52, 54-57, 100, 101, 146, 159, 182.
Dennis, W. C., 178.

Economic Problems, China, 159-161.
Education, 162-163.

Election laws, 4, 157.
England. See Great Britain.
Exterritoriality, 78, 105, 165 f.

Feng Kwo-chang, 42, 45, 95, 97-98, 101, 155.
Five-Power loan, 4.
Formosa, 7, 103.
France, Lao-hsi-kai incident, 63, 64, 83; possessions in China, 103-105.
Fukien, 21.

Germany, receives ultimatum from Japan, 9; war with Japan, 10; loses Tsingtao, 10; rights in Shantung taken by Japan, 14; rights at Peace Conference, 59-78; diplomatic relations severed by China, 59 ff., 67 ff.; China's note concerning submarine warfare, 68-69; the answer, 73; Kaiser's speech in 1900, 75; reasons for China's declaration of war, 72 ff.; arguments against, 81-84; declaration of war, 101; ousted from China, 149 ff.; Terauchi on Japanese Alliance, 177.
Goodnow, Dr. F. J., 5, 32, 83.
Great Britain, opium war, 82; adviser against dissolving parliament, 94; possessions in China, 103-105; supports open-door policy, 106; affected by Ishii Agreement, 120; war aims quoted, 153.

Hangchow, 50.
Hanyehping, Iron Company, 18.

Hara Takashi, 178.
Hay, Secretary, 102, 106, 182. See Open Door.
Hongkong, 83, 103.
Hornbeck, S. K., on Twenty-one Demands, 22, 23; on Open Door situation in 1915, 109; on revision of treaties with China, 171; on Allied financial policy in China, 175-176.
Howe, W. S., 146.
Hsu Shih-chang, 92, 156-158.
Hsuan Tung, 95.
Hung Hsien Dynasty, 39.

Ishii, Viscount, 102 ff., 124, 125, Appendix III.
Italy, 104.

Japan, growth and power, 7-8; ultimatum to Germany, 9; declaration of war against Germany, 9; disclaims territorial ambitions, 9-10; capture of Tsingtao, 10; new aims as result of world-war, 11; Twenty-one Demands, 2, 11, 13-23, 72, 78, 109, 123, 128, 165, 169, 180; Appendix II; boycott by China, 26; relation to Chinese monarchical movement, 37; feared by China, 81, 82, 149; attitude toward American advice, 94; adviser on parliament, 94; relations with Russia, 108; attitude toward Lansing-Ishii agreement, 124, 125; military agreement with China, 127 ff.; terms of agreement, 139-142; relation to Allied

ideal, 146; Terauchi on alliance with Germany, 177.
Japan Advertiser, 142, 143–144.

Kaiser, Wilhelm II, 75.
Kang Yu-wei, 84, 85, 95.
Kato, 12.
Kiaochow, 13, 80, 104.
Kinnosuke, Adachi, 112, 125.
Koo, V. K. Wellington, on China's contribution to Allies, 151–152; on Allied ideals in the Orient, 153; on United States' relations with China, 154, 155; on China's future, 164–166.
Korea, 7, 85, 103, 108, 118, Appendix V.
Kun Yuan Pao, 71, 72.

Labor Battalions, Chinese, in France, 150–151.
Lang Fang, 96.
Lansing, Secretary, 110 ff.; on Ishii agreement, 125–126. See Lansing-Ishii Agreement.
Lansing - Ishii Agreement, 102 ff.; reasons for, 110–113; notes exchanged, 113–116; supplementary statement, 116; criticism of agreement, 117–121; Chinese attitude, 122–124, Appendix III; Japanese attitude, 124–125; American attitude, 126, Appendix III.
Lao-hsi-tai incident, 63–64, 83.
Leases, 104.
Li Ching-hsi, 89.
Li Hung Chang, 89.
Li Yuan-hung, 4, 41, 44, 45, 52, 77, 90, 91, 94, 96, 98.
Liang Chi-chao, 42, 68, 80, 81, 96.

Liang Shih-yi, 95, 132, 156.
Liaotung Peninsula, 7, 104.
Lu Cheng-hsiang, 36.
Lu Yuang-ting, 158.

Manchu, 3, 95, 97.
Manchuria, 7, 8, 15–17, 59, 61–63, 103, 108, 109.
Mason, 177.
Millard's Review, on duty of the United States in China, 100, 101, 173, 174; terms of Sino-Japanese military agreement, 139–142; prize-list of books, 252 f.
Min-kwo-hsin-pao, 54–55.
Mission schools, 163.
Monarchical movement, 32 ff.
Monarchical society, 33 ff.
Mongolia, 7, 15, 17, 61–63, 108, 109.
Morrison, Dr., 31.
Motono, 134 ff.
Mukden, 62–63.
Murdock, Victor, 57.

Nanking, 3, 4, 5, 40, 42, 155.
National Convention Bureau, 35.
National Salvation Fund, 26.
Ni Shih-chung, 89.

Okuma, Count, 9, 10.
Open Door, 83, 102 ff., 106, 107, 108, 121, 126, 165, 166, 169, Appendices, II, F; IV and V.
Opium trade, 82, 159.
Opium War, 103.
Otani, General, 144.
Outlook, The, 177.

Parliament, 3, 5, 42, 45, 86, 88, 94.

Parliament, northern, 156.
Parliament, southern, 158.
Parties, 3, 79, 93, 158 ff.
Peace, conference, 24, 59, 72, 78, 147–149, 153, 163, 167, 171.
Peking, 95 ff., 133, 155.
Peking Gazette, on retirement of Yuan, 43; on severance of relations with Germany, 71; on war with Germany, 85; accuses Premier of "selling China, 87, 129–130.
Peking Jih-pao, 55–56.
Port Arthur, 7, 104, 108.
Portsmouth Treaty, 108, 121.
Postal service, 104–105.
Protocol of 1901, 96.
Provincial self-government, 52.
Putnam-Weale, on monarchical plot, 31; on administration of Li Yuan-hung, 50, 56; on military governors, 89; on Twenty-one Demands, 129; on revision of Chinese treaties, 171.

Railroad concessions, 105.
Rebellion of 1913, 4.
Recognition of Chinese Republic, 4.
Reinsch, Dr., 79, 92.
Religion, state, 52–54.
Revolution of 1911, 3.
Russia, possessions and leases in China, 103–105; relations with Japan, 108, 121; situation in 1917, 112, 127, 128, 144; affected by Ishii Agreement, 120. See Manchuria and Mongolia.

Salt monopoly, 104, 105.
Shantung, 14, 78, 104.

Siberia, 127, 144.
Spanish-American War, 106.
Spheres of interest, 104–105. See Open Door.
Sun Yat-sen, 3, 4, 158.
Sun Yu-chun, 32.
Sung Chiao-jen, 4.

Tang Chi-yao, 39, 90, 91.
Tang Shao-yi, 158.
Terauchi, Premier, 81–82, 177.
Tongking, 103.
Tsai Ao, 37, 41.
Tseng Chun-hsuan, 158.
Tsingtao, 10, 81, 104. See Kiaochow, and Shantung.
Tuan Chi-jui, 45, 76, 86, 87, 88, 96, 129–130, 155.
Twenty-one Demands, 2, 11, 13 ff., 72, 78, 87, 109, 123, 128–129, 165, 169, 180, Appendices I and II.
Twenty-four Demands, 21, Appendix II.
Tyau, M. T. Z., 152, 153, 170.

United States, recognition of Chinese Republic, 4; protest against Twenty-one Demands, 24, 123; influence on China's relations with Germany, 60, 78, 79; peace inquiry, 64; China's reply, 65–66; severance of relations with Germany, 67; Chinese note concerning similar action, 70; note to China on internal dissensions, 93–94 111; "sells" railroad concession, 105; treaty relations with China, 105, 106; Open Door policy,— see above; sends

troops to Siberia, 144; relations with China, 154–155.
Ussuri River, 103.

Vladivostok, 103, 127.

Wang, C. T., 51, 87, 89, 99, 158, 173–175.
Wang, Yi-tang, 156.
Waldersee, Wei-Hai-Wei, 104; Count, 74.
Weyl, Walter E., 161–162.
Williams, F. W., 147.
Wilson, President, 64, 145 ff., 167–176, 178–181. See United States.
World War, effects in Orient, 1–2; situation in China at its outbreak, 6; situation in Japan, 6–8; Japan declares war on Germany, 9; capture of Tsingtao, 10; new aims,

11 f.; China's severance of relations with Germany, 59 ff.; declaration of war against Germany, 72 ff., 101; Allied ideals in Asia, 145–147, 176 ff., 178, 181; China's contribution to Allies, 149–152; Japanese foreign policy resulting from war, Appendix I. See Germany, United States, Japan, Russia.
Wu Ting-fang, 41, 88, 94, 97, 98, 99, 158, 170, 171.

Yang Shan-teh, 50.
Yang Tu, 28–30.
Yangtze Valley, 104, 155.
Yuko Hanuguchi, 142, 143.
Yoshimoto, 61, 63.
Yuan Shih-kai, 3, 4, 5, 30, 31 ff., 38, 41, 44, 83.
Yunnan.

The Development of Japan

By KENNETH SCOTT LATOURETTE

Cloth, 12°

Japan in World Politics

By K. K. KAWAKAMI

Cloth, 12°, $1.50

" Not often does one find a discussion of Japanese and American relations that will compare with this little book in sanity, reasonableness, judicial temper, and ability to see the rights and wrongs of all sides of a question. It ought to be studied with care by all those jingoistic and fear-flustered Americans who break out every now and then into speech or print with wild outcries about what they insist is the Japanese menace. The pages are eloquent in their earnest pleading and sturdily honest and downright in their sense of the justice of their cause."—*N. Y. Times.*

" Few men have a clearer insight into the problems raised by the relations between the United States, Japan and China than K. K. Kawakami. . . . It will do any American good to read *Japan in World Politics,* who apparently regards a settlement of the far eastern problem as an essential preliminary to the general disarmament for which mankind longs."—*San Francisco Chronicle.*

Japanese Expansion and American Policies

By JAMES FRANCIS ABBOTT

Cloth, 12°, $1.50

" So much talk perfervid with alarm over the Japanese bogy is constantly blowing up and down this country that Prof. Abbott's calm-eyed and reasonably-minded book is, in comparison, like a cool and refreshing zephyr after a monsoon. . . . Just such a calm and sane looking in the face of facts and treating them in a reasonable way as the Japanese situation needs."—*N. Y. Times.*

" A sober and well-reasoned study . . . presents a sympathetic account of the development of Japan in the Meiji era, points out her present problems, and finds their solution in the industrial and commercial field, with China as her most vital market. He sees no danger in our relations with Japan, unless we provoke it."—*The Dial.*

THE MACMILLAN COMPANY

Publishers   64-66 Fifth Avenue   New York

LaVergne, TN USA
20 January 2010
170587LV00001B/221/A